12 SERMONS ON THE "CRIES FROM THE CROSS"

Charles H. Spurgeon

BAKER BOOK HOUSE

Grand Rapids, Michigan 49506

Reprinted 1982 by
Baker Book House
from the edition issued by
Passmore & Alabaster

ISBN: 0-8010-8223-4

PHOTOLITHOPRINTED BY CUSHING - MALLOY, INC.
ANN ARBOR, MICHIGAN, UNITED STATES OF AMERICA

Contents

1. The First Cry from the Cross

"Then said Jesus, Father, forgive them; for they know not what they do."—
[Luke xxiii. 34.

OUR Lord was at that moment enduring the first pains of crucifixion; the executioners had just then driven the nails through his hands and feet. He must have been, moreover, greatly depressed, and brought into a condition of extreme weakness by the agony of the night in Gethsemane, and by the scourgings and cruel mockings which he had endured all through the morning, from Caiaphas, Pilate, Herod, and the Prætorian guards. Yet neither the weakness of the past, nor the pain of the present, could prevent him from continuing in prayer. The Lamb of God was silent to men, but he was not silent to God. Dumb as a sheep before her shearers, he had not a word to say in his own defence to man, but he continues in his heart crying unto his Father, and no pain and no weakness can silence his holy supplications. Beloved, what an example our Lord herein presents to us! Let us continue in prayer so long as our heart beats; let no excess of suffering drive us away from the throne of grace, but rather let it drive us closer to it.

"Long as they live should Christians pray,
For only while they pray they live."

To cease from prayer is to renounce the consolations which our case requires. Under all distractions of spirit, and overwhelmings of heart, great God, help us still to pray, and never from the mercy-seat may our footsteps be driven by despair. Our blessed Redeemer persevered in prayer even when the cruel iron rent his tender nerves, and blow after blow of the hammer jarred his whole frame with anguish; and this perseverance may be accounted for by the fact that he was so in the habit of prayer that he could not cease from it; he had acquired a mighty velocity of intercession which forbade him to pause. Those long nights upon the cold mountain side, those many days which had been spent in solitude, those perpetual ejaculations which he was wont to dart up to heaven, all these had formed in him a habit so powerful, that the severest torments could not stay its force. Yet it was more than habit. Our Lord was baptised in the spirit of prayer; he lived in it, it lived in him, it had come to be an element of his nature. He was like that precious spice, which, being bruised, doth not cease to give forth its perfume, but rather yieldeth it all the more abundantly because of the blows of the pestle, its fragrance being no outward and superficial quality, but an inward virtue essential to its nature, which the pounding in the mortar did but fetch from it, causing it to reveal its secret soul of sweetness. So Jesus prays, even as a bundle of myrrh gives forth its smell, or as birds sing because they cannot do otherwise. Prayer enwrapped his very soul as with a garment, and his heart went forth in such array. I repeat it, let this be our example—never, under any circumstances, however severe the trial, or depressing the difficulty, let us cease from prayer.

Observe, further, that our Lord, in the prayer before us, remains in the vigour of faith as to his Sonship The extreme trial to which he now submitted himself could not prevent his holding fast his Sonship. His prayer begins, "Father." It was not without meaning that he taught us when we pray to say, "Our Father," for our prevalence in prayer will much depend upon our confidence in our relationship to God. Under great losses and crosses, one is apt to think that God is not dealing with us as a father with a child, but rather as a severe judge with a condemned criminal; but the cry of Christ, when he is brought to an extremity which we shall never reach, betrays no faltering in the spirit of sonship. In Gethsemane, when the bloody sweat fell fast upon the ground, his bitterest cry commenced with, "*My Father*," asking that if it were possible the cup of gall might pass from him; he pleaded with the Lord as his Father, even as he over and over again had called him on that dark and doleful night. Here, again, in this, the first of his seven expiring cries, it is "Father." O that the Spirit that makes us cry, "Abba, Father," may never cease his operations! May we never be brought into spiritual bondage by the suggestion, "If thou be the Son of God;" or if the tempter should so assail us, may we triumph as Jesus did in the hungry wilderness. May the Spirit which crieth, "Abba, Father," repel each unbelieving fear. When we are chastened, as we must be (for what son is there whom his father chasteneth not?) may we be in loving subjection to the Father of our spirits, and live; but never may we become captives to the spirit of bondage, so as to doubt the love of our gracious Father, or our share in his adoption.

More remarkable, however, is the fact that our Lord's prayer to his Father was not for himself. He continued on the cross to pray for himself, it is true, and his lamentable cry, "My God, my God, why hast thou forsaken me?" shows the personality of his prayer; but the first of the seven great cries on the cross has scarcely even an indirect reference to himself. It is, "Father, forgive *them*." The petition is altogether for others, and though there is an allusion to the cruelties which they were exercising upon himself, yet it is remote; and you will observe, he does not say, "I forgive them"—that is taken for granted—he seems to lose sight of the fact that they were doing any wrong to himself, it is the wrong which they were doing to the Father that is on his mind, the insult which they are paying to the Father, in the person of the Son; he thinks not of himself at all. The cry, "Father, forgive them," is altogether unselfish. He himself is, in the prayer, as though he were not; so complete is his self-annihilation, that he loses sight of himself and his woes. My brethren, if there had ever been a time in the life of the Son of man when he might have rigidly confined his prayer to himself, without any one cavilling thereat, surely it was when he was beginning his death throes. We could not marvel, if any man here were fastened to the stake, or fixed to a cross, if his first, and even his last and all his prayers, were for support under so arduous a trial. But see, the Lord Jesus began his prayer by pleading for others. See ye not what a great heart is here revealed! What a soul of compassion was in the Crucified! How Godlike, how divine! Was there ever such a one before him, who, even in the very pangs of death, offers as his first prayer an intercession for others? Let this unselfish spirit be in you also, my brethren. Look not every man upon his own things, but every man also on the things of others. Love your neighbours as yourselves, and as Christ has set before you this paragon of unselfishness, seek to follow him, treading in his steps.

There is, however, a crowning jewel in this diadem of glorious love. The Sun of Righteousness sets upon Calvary in a wondrous splendour; but amongst the bright colours which glorify his departure, there is this one—the prayer was not alone for others, but it was for his cruellest enemies. His enemies, did I say, there is more than that to be considered. It was not a prayer for enemies who had done him an ill deed years before, but for those who were there and then murdering him. Not in cold blood did the Saviour pray, after he had forgotten the injury, and could the more easily forgive it, but while the first red drops of blood were spurting on the hands which drove the nails; while yet the hammer was bestained with crimson gore, his blessed mouth poured out the fresh warm prayer, "Father, forgive them, for they know not what they do." I say, not that that prayer was confined to his immediate executioners. I believe that it was a far-reaching prayer, which included Scribes and Pharisees, Pilate and Herod, Jews and Gentiles—yea, the whole human race in a certain sense, since we were all concerned in that murder; but certainly the immediate persons, upon whom that prayer was poured like precious nard, were those who there and then were committing the brutal act of fastening him to the accursed tree. How sublime is this prayer if viewed in such a light! It stands alone upon a mount of solitary glory. No other had been prayed like it before. It is true, Abraham, and Moses, and the prophets had prayed for the wicked; but not for wicked men who had pierced their hands and feet. It is true, that Christians have since that day offered the same prayer, even as Stephen cried, " Lay not this sin to their charge;" and many a martyr has made his last words at the stake words of pitying intercession for his persecutors; but you know where they learnt this, let me ask you where did *he* learn it? Was not Jesus the divine original? He learnt it nowhere; it leaped up from his own Godlike nature. A compassion peculiar to himself dictated this originality of prayer; the inward royalty of his love suggested to him so memorable an intercession, which may serve us for a pattern, but of which no pattern had existed before. J feel as though I could better kneel before my Lord's cross at this moment than stand in this pulpit to talk to you. I want to adore him; I worship him in heart for that prayer; if I knew nothing else of him but this one prayer, I must adore him, for that one matchless plea for mercy convinces me most overwhelmingly of the deity of him who offered it, and fills my heart with reverent affection.

Thus have I introduced to you our Lord's first vocal prayer upon the cross. I shall now, if we are helped by God's Holy Spirit, make some use of it. First, we shall view it as *illustrative of our Saviour's intercession;* secondly, we shall regard the text as *instructive of the church's work;* thirdly, we shall consider it as *suggestive to the unconverted.*

I. First, my dear brethren, let us look at this very wonderful text as ILLUSTRATIVE OF OUR LORD'S INTERCESSION.

He prayed for his enemies then, he is praying for his enemies now; the past on the cross was an earnest of the present on the throne. He is in a higher place, and in a nobler condition, but his occupation is the same; he continues still before the eternal throne to present pleas on the behalf of guilty men, crying, "Father, O forgive them." All his intercession is in a measure like the intercession on Calvary, and Calvary's cries may help us to guess the character of the whole of his intercession above.

The first point in which we may see the character of his intercession is this—it is *most gracious.* Those for whom our Lord prayed, according to the text, did not deserve his prayer. They had done nothing which could call forth from him a benediction as a reward for their endeavours in his service ; on the contrary, they were most undeserving persons, who had conspired to put him to death. They had crucified him, crucified him wantonly and malignantly; they were even then taking away his innocent life. His clients were persons who, so far from being meritorious, were utterly undeserving of a single good wish from the Saviour's heart. They certainly never asked him to pray for them—it was the last thought in their minds to say, "Intercede for us, thou dying King! Offer petitions on our behalf, thou Son of God!" I will venture to believe the prayer itself, when they heard it, was either disregarded, and passed over with contemptuous indifference, or perhaps it was caught at as a theme for jest. I admit that it seems to be too severe upon humanity to suppose it possible that such a prayer could have been the theme for laughter, and yet there were other things enacted around the cross which were quite as brutal, and I can imagine that this also might have happened. Yet our Saviour prayed for persons who did not deserve the prayer, but, on the contrary, merited a curse—persons who did not ask for the prayer, and even scoffed at it when they heard it. Even so in heaven there stands the great High Priest, who pleads for guilty men—for *guilty* men, my hearers. There are none on earth that deserve his intercession. He pleads for none on the supposition that they do deserve it. He stands there to plead as the just One on the behalf of the unjust. Not if any man be righteous, but "if any man sin, we have an advocate with the Father." Remember, too, that our great Intercessor pleads for such as never asked him to plead for them. His elect, while yet dead in trespasses and sins, are the objects of his compassionate intercessions, and while they even scoff at his gospel, his heart of love is entreating the favour of heaven on their behalf. See, then, beloved, if such be the truth, how sure you are to speed with God who earnestly ask the Lord Jesus Christ to plead for you. Some of you, with many tears and much earnestness, have been beseeching the Saviour to be your advocate ? Will he refuse you ? Stands it to reason that he can ? He pleads for those that reject his pleadings, much more for you who prize them beyond gold. Remember, my dear hearer, if there be nothing good in you, and if there be everything conceivable that is malignant and bad, yet none of these things can be any barrier to prevent Christ's exercising the office of Intercessor for you. Even for you he will plead. Come, put your case into his hands; for you he will find pleas which you cannot discover for yourselves, and he will put the case to God for you as for his murderers, " Father, forgive them."

A second quality of his intercession is this—*its careful spirit.* You notice in the prayer, " Father, forgive them, for they know not what they do." Our Saviour did, as it were, look his enemies through and through to find something in them that he could urge in their favour; but he could see nothing until his wisely affectionate eye lit upon their ignorance : " they know not what they do." How carefully he surveyed the circumstances, and the characters of those for whom he importuned! Just so it is with him in heaven. Christ is no careless advocate for his people. He knows your precise condition at this moment, and the exact state of your heart with regard to the temptation through which you are passing; more than that, he foresees the temptation which is awaiting you, and in his intercession he takes note of the future event which his prescient eye beholds. " Satan hath desired to have thee, that he may sift thee as wheat; but I have prayed for thee that thy faith fail not." Oh, the condescending tenderness of our great High Priest! He knows us better than we know ourselves. He understands every secret grief and groaning. You need not trouble yourself about the wording of your prayer, he will put the wording right. And even the understanding as to the exact petition, if you should fail in it, he cannot, for as he knoweth what is the mind of God, so he knoweth what is your mind also. He can spy out some reason for mercy in you which you cannot detect in yourselves, and when it is so dark and cloudy with your soul that you cannot discern a foothold for a plea that you may urge with heaven, the Lord Jesus has the pleas ready framed, and petitions ready drawn up, and he can present them acceptable before the mercy-seat. His intercession, then, you will observe is very gracious, and in the next place it is very thoughtful.

We must next note its *earnestness.* No one doubts who reads these words, "Father, forgive them, for they know not what they do," that they were heaven-piercing in their fervour. Brethren, you are certain, even without a thought, that Christ was terribly in earnest in that prayer. But there is an argument to prove that. Earnest people are usually witty, and quick of understanding, to discover anything which may serve their turn. If you are pleading for life, and an argument for your being spared be asked of you, I will warrant you that you will think of one when no one else might. Now, Jesus was so in earnest for the salvation of his enemies, that he struck upon an argument for mercy which a less anxious spirit would not have thought of: "They know not what they do." Why, sirs, that was in strictest justice but a scant reason for mercy; and indeed, ignorance, if it be wilful, does not extenuate sin, and yet the ignorance of many who surrounded the cross was a wilful ignorance. They might have known that he was the Lord of glory. Was not Moses plain enough? Had not Esaias been very bold in his speech? Were not the signs and tokens such that one might as well doubt which is the sun in the firmament as the claims of Jesus to be the Messias? Yet, for all that, the Saviour, with marvellous earnestness and consequent dexterity, turns what might not have been a plea into a plea, and puts it thus: "Father, forgive them, *for* they know not what they do." Oh, how mighty are his pleas in heaven, then, in their earnestness! Do not suppose that he is less quick of understanding there, or less intense in the vehemence of his entreaties. No, my brethren, the heart of Christ still labours with the eternal God. He is no slumbering intercessor, but, for Zion's sake, he doth not hold his peace, and for Jerusalem's sake, he doth not cease, nor will he, till her righteousness go forth as brightness, and her salvation as a lamp that burneth.

It is interesting to note, in the fourth place, that the prayer here offered helps us to judge of his intercession in heaven as to its *continuance*, perseverance, and perpetuity. As I remarked before, if our Saviour might have paused from intercessory prayer, it was surely when they fastened him to the tree; when they were guilty of direct acts of deadly violence to his divine person, he might then have ceased to present petitions on their behalf. But sin cannot tie the tongue of our interceding Friend. Oh, what comfort is here! You have sinned, believer, you have grieved his Spirit, but you have not stopped that potent tongue which pleads for you. You have been unfruitful, perhaps, my brother, and like the barren tree, you deserve to be cut down; but your want of fruitfulness has not withdrawn the Intercessor from his place. He interposes at this moment, crying, "Spare it yet another year." Sinner, you have provoked God by long rejecting his mercy and going from bad to worse, but neither blasphemy nor unrighteousness, nor infidelity, shall stay the Christ of God from urging the suit of the very chief of sinners. He lives, and while he lives he pleads; and while there is a sinner upon earth to be saved, there shall be an intercessor in heaven to plead for him. These are but fragments of thought, but they will help you, I hope, to realise the intercession of your great High Priest.

Think yet again, this prayer of our Lord on earth is like his prayer in heaven, because of its *wisdom*. He seeks the best thing, and that which his clients most need, "Father, *forgive* them." That was the great point in hand; they wanted most of all there and then forgiveness from God. He does not say, "Father, enlighten them, for they know not what they do," for mere enlightenment would but have created torture of conscience and hastened on their hell; but he crieth, "Father, forgive;" and while he used his voice, the precious drops of blood which were then distilling from the nail wounds were pleading too, and God heard, and doubtless did forgive. The first mercy which is needful to guilty sinners is forgiven sin. Christ wisely prays for the boon most wanted. It is so in heaven; he pleads wisely and prudently. Let him alone, he knows what to ask for at the divine hand. Go you to the mercy-seat, and pour out your desires as best you can, but when you have done so always put it thus, " O my Lord Jesus, answer no desire of mine if it be not according to thy judgment ; and if in aught that I have asked I have failed to seek for what I want, amend my pleading, for thou art infinitely wiser than I." Oh, it is sweet to have a friend at court to perfect our petitions for us before they come unto the great King. I believe that there is never presented to God anything but a perfect prayer now; I mean, that before the great Father of us all, no prayer of his people ever comes up imperfect; there is nothing left out, and there is nothing to be erased; and this, not because their prayers were originally perfect in themselves, but because the Mediator makes them perfect through his infinite wisdom, and they come up before the mercy-seat moulded according to the mind of God himself, and he is sure to grant such prayers.

Once more, this memorable prayer of our crucified Lord was like to his universal intercession in the matter of its *prevalence.* Those for whom he prayed were many of them forgiven. Do you remember that he said to his disciples when he bade them preach, " beginning at Jerusalem," and on that day when Peter stood up with the eleven, and charged the people that with wicked hands they had crucified and slain the Saviour, three thousand of these persons who were thus justly accused of his crucifixion became believers in him, and were baptised in his name. That was an answer to Jesus' prayer. The priests were at the bottom of our Lord's murder, they were the most guilty ; but it is said, " a great company also of the priests believed." Here was another answer to the prayer. Since all men had their share representatively, Gentiles as well as Jews, in the death of Jesus, the gospel was soon preached to the Jews, and within a short time it was preached to the Gentiles also. Was not this prayer, "Father, forgive them," like a stone cast into a lake, forming at first a narrow circle, and then a wider ring, and soon a larger sphere, until the whole lake is covered with circling waves ? Such a prayer as this, cast into the whole world, first created a little ring of Jewish converts and of priests, and then a wider circle of such as were beneath the Roman sway ; and to-day its circumference is wide as the globe itself, so that tens of thousands are saved through the prevalence of this one intercessi on

"Father, forgive them." It is certainly so with him in heaven, he never pleads in vain. With bleeding hands, he yet won the day; with feet fastened to the wood, he was yet victorious; forsaken of God and despised of the people, he was yet triumphant in his pleas; how much more so now the tiara is about his brow, his hand grasps the universal sceptre, and his feet are shod with silver sandals, and he is crowned King of kings, and Lord of lords! If tears and cries out of weakness were omnipotent, even more mighty if possible must be that sacred authority which as the risen Priest he claims when he stands before the Father's throne to mention the covenant which the Father made with him. O ye trembling believers, trust him with your concerns! Come hither, ye guilty, and ask him to plead for you. O you that cannot pray, come, ask him to intercede for you. Broken hearts and weary heads, and disconsolate bosoms, come ye to him who into the golden censer will put his merits, and then place your prayers with them, so that they shall come up as the smoke of perfume, even as a fragrant cloud into the nostrils of the Lord God of hosts, who will smell a sweet savour, and accept you and your prayers in the Beloved. We have now opened up more than enough sea-room for your meditations at home this afternoon, and, therefore we leave this first point. We have had an illustration in the prayer of Christ on the cross of what his prayers always are in heaven.

II. Secondly, the text is INSTRUCTIVE OF THE CHURCH'S WORK.

As Christ was, so his church is to be in this world. Christ came into this world not to be ministered unto, but to minister, not to be honoured, but to save others. His church, when she understands her work, will perceive that she is not here to gather to herself wealth or honour, or to seek any temporal aggrandisement and position; she is here unselfishly to live, and if need be, unselfishly to die for the deliverance of the lost sheep, the salvation of lost men. Brethren, Christ's prayer on the cross I told you was altogether an unselfish one. He does not remember himself in it. Such ought to be the church's life-prayer, the church's active interposition on the behalf of sinners. She ought to live never for her ministers or for herself, but ever for the lost sons of men. Imagine you that churches are formed to maintain ministers? Do you conceive that the church exists in this land merely that so much salary may be given to bishops, and deans, and prebends, and curates, and I know not what? My brethren, it were well if the whole thing were abolished if that were its only aim. The aim of the church is not to provide out-door relief for the younger sons of the nobility; when they have not brains enough to win anyhow else their livelihood, they are stuck into family livings. Churches are not made that men of ready speech may stand up on Sundays and talk, and so win daily bread from their admirers. Nay, there is another end and aim from this. These places of worship are not built that you may sit here comfortably, and hear something that shall make you pass away your Sundays with pleasure. A church in London which does not exist to do good in the slums, and dens, and kennels of the city, is a church that has no reason to justify its longer existing. A church that does not exist to reclaim heathenism, to fight with evil, to destroy error, to put down falsehood, a church that does not exist to take the side of the poor, to denounce injustice and to hold up righteousness, is a church that has no right to be. Not for thyself, O church, dost thou exist, any more than Christ existed for himself. His glory was that he laid aside his glory, and the glory of the church is when she lays aside her respectability and her dignity, and counts it to be her glory to gather together the outcasts, and her highest honour to seek amid the foulest mire the priceless jewels for which Jesus shed his blood. To rescue souls from hell and lead to God, to hope, to heaven, this is her heavenly occupation. O that the church would always feel this ! Let her have her bishops and her preachers, and let them be supported, and let everything be done for Christ's sake decently and in order, but let the end be looked to, namely, the conversion of the wandering, the teaching of the ignorant, the help of the poor, the maintenance of the right, the putting down of the wrong, and the upholding at all hazards of the crown and kingdom of our Lord Jesus Christ.

Now the prayer of Christ had a *great spirituality of aim.* You notice that nothing is sought for these people but that which concerns their souls, "Father, *forgive* them." And I believe the church will do well when she recollects that she wrestles not with flesh and blood, nor with principalities and powers, but with spiritual wickedness, and that what she has to dispense is not the law and order by which magistrates may be upheld, or tyrannies pulled down, but the spiritual government by which hearts are conquered to Christ, and judgments are brought into subjection to his truth. I believe that the more the church of God strains after, before God, the forgiveness of sinners, and the more she seeks in her life prayer to teach sinners what sin is, and what the blood of Christ is, and what the hell that must follow if sin be not washed out, and what the heaven is which will be ensured to all those who are cleansed from sin, the more she keeps to this the better. Press forward as one man, my brethren, to secure the root of the matter in the forgiveness of sinners. As to all the evils that afflict humanity, by all means take your share in battling with them; let temperance be maintained, let education be supported; let reforms, political and ecclesiastical, be pushed forward as far as you have the time and effort to spare, but the first business of every Christian man and woman is with the hearts and consciences of men as they stand before the everlasting God. O let nothing turn you aside from your divine errand of mercy to undying

souls. This is your one business. Tell to sinners that sin will damn
them, that Christ alone can take away sin, and make this the one
passion of your souls, "Father, forgive them, forgive them! Let them
know how to be forgiven. Let them be actually forgiven, and let me
never rest except as I am the means of bringing sinners to be forgiven,
even the guiltiest of them."

Our Saviour's prayer teaches the church that while her spirit should
be unselfish, and her aim should be spiritual, *the range of her mission* is
to be unlimited. Christ prayed for the wicked, what if I say the most
wicked of the wicked, that ribald crew that had surrounded his cross!
He prayed for the ignorant. Doth he not say, "They know not what they
do"? He prayed for his persecutors; the very persons who were most
at enmity with him, lay nearest to his heart. Church of God, your
mission is not to the respectable few who will gather about your
ministers to listen respectfully to their words; your mission is not to
the *élite* and the eclectic, the intelligent who will criticise your words
and pass judgment upon every syllable of your teaching; your mission
is not to those who treat you kindly, generously, affectionately, not to
these I mean alone, though certainly to these as among the rest;
but your great errand is to the harlot, to the thief, to the swearer and
the drunkard, to the most depraved and debauched. If no one else
cares for these, the church always must, and if there be any who are first in
her prayers it should be these who alas! are generally last in our thoughts.
The ignorant we ought diligently to consider. It is not enough for the
preacher that he preaches so that those instructed from their youth up
can understand him; he must think of those to whom the commonest
phrases of theological truth are as meaningless as the jargon of an
unknown tongue; he must preach so as to reach the meanest compre-
hension; and if the ignorant many come not to hear him, he must use
such means as best he may to induce them, nay, compel them to hear
the good news. The gospel is meant also for those who persecute
religion; it aims its arrows of love against the hearts of its foes. If
there be any whom we should first seek to bring to Jesus, it should be
just these who are the farthest off and most opposed to the gospel of
Christ. "Father, forgive *them*; if thou dost pardon none besides, yet
be pleased to forgive *them*."

So, too, the church should be *earnest* as Christ was; and if she be so,
she will be quick to notice any ground of hope in those she deals with,
quick to observe any plea that she may use with God for their
salvation.

She must be *hopeful* too, and surely no church ever had a more
hopeful sphere than the church of this present age. If ignorance be
a plea with God, look on the heathen at this day—millions of them
never heard Messiah's name. Forgive them, great God, indeed they

know not what they do. If ignorance be some ground for hope, there is hope enough in this great city of London, for have we not around us hundreds of thousands to whom the simplest truths of the gospel would be the greatest novelties ? Brethren, it is sad to think that this country should still lie under such a pall of ignorance, but the sting of so dread a fact is blunted with hope when we read the Saviour's prayer aright—it helps us to hope while we cry, " Forgive them, for they know not what they do."

It is the church's business to seek after the most fallen and the most ignorant, and to seek them perseveringly. She should never stay her hand from doing good. If the Lord be coming to-morrow, it is no reason why you Christian people should subside into mere talkers and readers, meeting together for mutual comfort, and forgetting the myriads of perishing souls. If it be true that this world is going to pieces in a fortnight, and that Louis Napoleon is the Apocalyptic beast, or if it be not true, I care not a fig, it makes no difference to my duty, and does not change my service. Let my Lord come when he will, while I labour for him I am ready for his appearing. The business of the church is still to watch for the salvation of souls. If she stood gazing, as modern prophets would have her ; if she gave up her mission to indulge in speculative interpretations, she might well be afraid of her Lord's coming ; but if she goes about her work, and with incessant toil searches out her Lord's precious jewels, she shall not be ashamed when her Bridegroom cometh.

My time has been much too short for so vast a subject as I have undertaken, but I wish I could speak words that were as loud as thunder, with a sense and earnestness as mighty as the lightning. I would fain excite every Christian here, and kindle in him a right idea of what his work is as a part of Christ's church. My brethren, you must not live to yourselves; the accumulation of money, the bringing up of your children, the building of houses, the earning of your daily bread, all this you may do; but there must be a greater object than this if you are to be Christlike, as you should be, since you are bought with Jesus' blood. Begin to live for others, make it apparent unto all men that you are not yourselves the end-all and be-all of your own existence, but that you are spending and being spent, that through the good you do to men God may be glorified, and Christ may see in you his own image and be satisfied.

III. Time fails me, but the last point was to be a word SUGGESTIVE TO THE UNCONVERTED.

Listen attentively to these sentences. I will make them as terse and condensed as possible. Some of you here are not saved. Now, some of you have been very ignorant, and when you sinned you did not know what you did. You knew you were sinners, you knew that, but you did not know the far-reaching guilt of sin. You have not been attending the house of prayer long, you have not read your Bible, you have not Christian parents. Now you are beginning to be anxious about your souls. Remember your ignorance does not excuse you, or else Christ would not say, "Forgive them;" they must be forgiven, even those that know not what they do, hence they are individually guilty; but still that ignorance of yours gives you just a little gleam of hope. The times of your ignorance God winked at, but now commandeth all men everywhere to repent. Bring forth, therefore, fruits meet for repentance. The God whom you have ignorantly forgotten is willing to pardon and ready to forgive. The gospel is just this, trust Jesus Christ who died for the guilty, and you shall be saved. O may God help you to do so this very morning, and you will become new men and new women, a change will take place in you equal to a new birth; you will be new creatures in Christ Jesus.

But ah! my friends, there are some here for whom even Christ himself could not pray this prayer, in the widest sense at any rate, "Father, forgive them; for they know not what they do," for you have known what you did, and every sermon you hear, and especially every impression that is made upon your understanding and conscience by the gospel, adds to your responsibility, and takes away from you the excuse of not knowing what you do. Ah! sirs, you know that there is the world and Christ, and that you cannot have both. You know that there is sin and God, and that you cannot serve both. You know that there are the pleasures of evil and the pleasures of heaven, and that you cannot have both. Oh! in the light which God has given you, may his Spirit also come and help you to choose that which true wisdom would make you choose. Decide to-day for God, for Christ, for heaven. The Lord decide you for his name's sake. Amen.

2. Christ's Plea
for Ignorant Sinners

"Then said Jesus, Father, forgive them; for they know not what they do."—
Luke xxiii. 34.

WHAT tenderness we have here; what self-forgetfulness; what almighty love! Jesus did not say to those who crucified him, "Begone!" One such word, and they must have all fled. When they came to take him in the garden, they went backward, and fell to the ground, when he spoke but a short sentence; and now that he is on the cross, a single syllable would have made the whole company fall to the ground, or flee away in fright.

Jesus says not a word in his own defence. When he prayed to his Father, he might justly have said, "Father, note what they do to thy beloved Son. Judge them for the wrong they do to him who loves them, and who has done all he can for them." But there is no prayer against them in the words that Jesus utters. It was written of old, by the prophet Isaiah, "He made intercession for the transgressors;" and here it is fulfilled. He pleads for his murderers, "Father, forgive them."

He does not utter a single word of upbraiding. He does not say, "Why do ye this? Why pierce the hands that fed you? Why nail the feet that followed after you in mercy? Why mock the Man who loved to bless you?" No; not a word even of gentle upbraiding, much less of anything like a curse. "Father, forgive them." You notice, Jesus does not say, "I forgive them," but you may read that between the lines. He says that all the more because he does not say it in words. But he has laid aside his majesty, and is fastened to the cross; and therefore he takes the humble position of a suppliant, rather than the more lofty place of one who had power to forgive. How often, when men say, "I forgive you," is there a kind of selfishness about it! At any rate, self is asserted in the very act of forgiving. Jesus takes the place of a pleader, a pleader for those who were committing murder upon himself. Blessed be his name!

This word of the cross we shall use to-night, and we shall see if we cannot gather something from it for our instruction; for, though we were not there, and we did not actually put Jesus to death, yet we really caused his death, and we, too, crucified the Lord of glory; and his prayer for us was, "Father, forgive them; for they know not what they do."

I am not going to handle this text so much by way of exposition, as by way of experience. I believe there are many here, to whom these words will be very appropriate. This will be our line of thought. First, *we were in measure ignorant;* secondly, *we confess that this ignorance is no excuse;* thirdly, *we bless our Lord for pleading for us;* and fourthly, *we now rejoice in the pardon we have obtained.* May the Holy Spirit graciously help us in our meditation!

I. Looking back upon our past experience, let me say, first, that WE WERE IN MEASURE IGNORANT. We who have been forgiven, we who have been washed in the blood of the Lamb, we once sinned, in a great measure, through ignorance. Jesus says, "They know not what they do." Now, I shall appeal to you, brothers and sisters, when you lived under the dominion of Satan, and served yourselves and sin, was there not a measure of ignorance in it? You can truly say, as we said in the hymn we sang just now,—

"Alas! I knew not what I did."

It is true, first, that we were ignorant of *the awful meaning of sin.* We began to sin as children; we knew that it was wrong, but we did not know all that sin meant. We went on to sin as young men; peradventure we plunged into much wickedness. We knew it was wrong; but we did not see the end from the beginning. It did not appear to us as rebellion against God. We did not think that we were presumptuously defying God, setting at naught his wisdom, defying his power, deriding his love, spurning his holiness; yet we were doing all that. There is an abysmal depth in sin. You cannot see to the bottom of it. When we rolled sin under our tongue as a sweet morsel, we did not know all the terrible ingredients compounded in that deadly bittersweet. We were in a measure ignorant of the tremendous crime we committed when we dared to live in rebellion against God. So far, I think, you go with me.

We did not know, at that time, *God's great love to us.* I did not know that he had chosen me from before the foundation of the world; I never dreamed of that. I did not know that Christ stood for me as my Substitute, to redeem me from among men. I did not know that he had espoused me unto himself in righteousness and in faithfulness, to be one with him for ever. You, dear friends, who now know the love of Christ, did not understand it then. You did not know that you were sinning against eternal love, against infinite compassion, against a distinguishing love such as God had fixed on you from eternity. So far, we knew not what we did.

I think, too, that we did not know all that we were doing in *our rejection of Christ, and putting him to grief.* He came to us in our youth; and impressed by a sermon we began to tremble, and to seek his face; but we were decoyed back to the world, and we refused Christ. Our mother's tears, our father's prayers, our teacher's admonitions, often moved us; but we were very stubborn, and we rejected Christ. We did not know that, in that rejection, we were virtually putting him away and crucifying him. We were denying his Godhead, or else we should have worshipped him. We were denying his love, or else we should have yielded to him. We were practically, in every act of sin, taking the hammer and the nails, and fastening Christ to the cross; but we did not know it. Perhaps, if we had known it, we should not have crucified the Lord of glory. We did know we were doing wrong; but we did not know all the wrong that we were doing.

Nor did we know fully *the meaning of our delays.* We hesitated; we were on the verge of conversion; we went back, and turned again to our old follies. We were hardened, Christless, prayerless still; and each one of us said, "Oh, I am only waiting a little while till I have fulfilled my present engagements, till I am a little older, till I have seen a little more of the world!" The fact is, we were refusing Christ, and choosing the pleasures of sin instead of him; and every hour of delay was an hour of crucifying Christ, grieving his Spirit, and choosing this harlot world in the place of the lovely and ever-blessed Christ. We did not know that.

I think we may add one thing more. *We did not know the meaning of our self-righteousness.* We used to think, some of us, that we had a righteousness of our own. We had been to church regularly, or we had been to the meeting-house whenever it was open. We were christened; we were confirmed; or, peradventure, we rejoiced that we never had either of those things done to us. Thus, we put our confidence in ceremonies, or the absence of ceremonies. We said our prayers; we read a chapter in the Bible night and morning; we did —oh, I do not know what we did not do! But there we rested; we were righteous in our own esteem. We had not any particular sin to confess, nor any reason to lie in the dust before the throne of God's majesty. We were about as good as we could be; and we did not know that we were even then perpetrating the highest insult upon Christ; for, if we were not sinners, why did Christ die; and, if we had a righteousness of our own which was good enough, why did Christ come here to work out a righteousness for us? We made out Christ to be a superfluity, by considering that we were good enough without resting in his atoning sacrifice. Ah, we did not think we were doing that! We thought we were pleasing God by our religiousness, by our outward performances, by our ecclesiastical correctness; but all the while we were setting up anti-Christ in the place of Christ. We were making out that Christ was not wanted; we were robbing him of his office and glory! Alas! Christ could say of us, with regard to all these things, "They know not what they do." I want you to look quietly at the time past wherein you served sin, and just see whether there was not a darkness upon your mind, a blindness in your spirit, so that you did not know what you did.

II. Well now, secondly, WE CONFESS THAT THIS IGNORANCE IS NO EXCUSE. Our Lord might urge it as a plea; but we never could. We did not know what we did, and so we were not guilty to the fullest possible extent; but we were guilty enough, therefore let us own it.

For first, remember, *the law never allows this as a plea.* **In our own** English law, a man is supposed to know what the law is. If he breaks it, it is no excuse to plead that he did not know it. It may be regarded by a judge as some extenuation; but the law allows nothing of the kind. God gives us the law, and we are bound to keep it. If I erred through not knowing the law, still it was a sin. Under the Mosaic law, there were sins of ignorance, and for these there were special offerings. The ignorance did not blot out the sin. That is clear in my text; for, if ignorance rendered an action no longer sinful, then why should Christ say, "Father, forgive them"? But he does; he asks for mercy for what is sin, even though the ignorance in some measure be supposed to mitigate the criminality of it.

But, dear friends, *we might have known.* If we did not know, it was because we would not know. There was the preaching of the Word; but we did not care to hear it. There was this blessed Book; but we did not care to read it. If you and I had sat down, and looked at our conduct by the light of Holy Scripture, we might have known much more of the evil of sin, and much more of the love of Christ, and much more of the ingratitude which is possible in refusing Christ, and not coming to him.

In addition to that, *we did not think.* "Oh, but," you say, "young people never do think!" But young people should think. If there is anybody who need not think, it is the old man, whose day is nearly over. If he does think, he has but a very short time in which to improve; but the young have all their life before them. If I were a carpenter, and had to make a box, I should not think about it after I had made the box; I should think, before I began to cut my timber, what sort of box it was to be. In every action, a man thinks before he begins, or else he is a fool. A young man ought to think more than anybody else, for now he is, as it were, making his box. He is beginning his life-plan; he should be the most thoughtful of all men. Many of us, who are now Christ's people, would have known much more about our Lord if we had given him more careful consideration in our earlier days. A man will consider about taking a wife, he will consider about taking a business, he will consider about buying a horse or a cow; but he will not consider about the claims of Christ, and the claims of the Most High God; and this renders his ignorance wilful, and inexcusable.

Beside that, dear friends, although we have confessed to ignorance, *in many sins we did know a great deal.* Come, let me quicken your memories. There were times when you knew that such an action was wrong, when you started back from it. You looked at the gain it would bring you, and you sold your soul for that price, and deliberately did what you were well aware was wrong. Are there not some here, saved by Christ, who must confess that, at times, they did violence to their conscience? They did despite to the Spirit of God, quenched the light of heaven, drove the Spirit away from them, distinctly knowing what they were doing. Let us bow before God in the silence of our hearts, and own to all this. We hear the Master say, "Father, forgive them; for they know not what they do." Let us add our own tears as we say, "And forgive us, also, because in some things we did know; in all things we might have known; but we were ignorant for want of thought, which thought was a solemn duty which we ought to have rendered to God."

One thing more I will say on this head. When a man is ignorant, and does not know what he ought to do, what should he do? Well, he should do nothing till he does know. But here is the mischief of it, that *when we did not know, yet we chose to do the wrong thing.* If we did not know, why did we not choose the right thing? But, being in the dark, we never turned to the right; but always blundered to the left, from sin to sin. Does not this show us how depraved our hearts are? Though we are seeking to be right, when we are let alone, we go wrong of ourselves. Leave a child alone; leave a man alone; leave a tribe alone without teaching and instruction; what comes of it? Why, the same as when you leave a field alone. It never, by any chance, produces wheat or barley. Leave it alone, and there are rank weeds, and thorns, and briars, showing that the natural set of the soil is towards producing that which is worthless. O friends, confess the innate evil of your hearts as well as the evil of your lives, in that, when you did not know, yet, having a perverse instinct, you chose the evil, and refused the good; and, when you did not know enough of Christ, and did not think enough of him to know whether you ought to have him or not, you would not come unto him that you might have life. You needed light; but you shut your eyes to the sun. You were thirsty; but you would not drink of the living spring; and so your ignorance, though it was there, was a criminal ignorance, which you must confess before the Lord. Oh, come ye to the cross, ye who have been there before, and have lost your burden there! Come and confess your guilt over again; and clasp that cross afresh, and look to him who bled upon it, and praise his dear name that he once prayed for you, " Father, forgive them; for they know not what they do."

Now, I am going a step further. We were in a measure ignorant; but we confess that that measurable ignorance was no excuse.

III. Now, thirdly, WE BLESS OUR LORD FOR PLEADING FOR US.

Do you notice when it was that Jesus pleaded? It was, *while they were crucifying him.* They had just driven in the nails, they had lifted up the cross, and dashed it down into its socket, and dislocated all his bones, so that he could say, " I am poured out like water, and all my bones are out of joint." Ah, dear friends, it was then that, instead of a cry or a groan, this dear Son of God said, " Father, forgive them; for they know not what they do." They did not ask forgiveness for themselves; Jesus asked forgiveness for them. Their hands were imbrued in his blood; and it was then, even then, that he prayed for them. Let us think of the great love wherewith he loved us, even while we were yet sinners, when we rioted in sin, when we drank it down as the ox drinketh down water. Even then he prayed for us. " While we were yet without strength, in due time Christ died for the ungodly." Bless his name to-night. He prayed for you when you did not pray for yourself. He prayed for you when you were crucifying him.

Then think of his plea, *he pleads his Sonship.* He says, " *Father,*

forgive them." He was the Son of God, and he puts his divine
Sonship into the scale on our behalf. He seems to say, "Father, as
I am thy Son, grant me this request, and pardon these rebels. Father,
forgive them." The filial rights of Christ were very great. He was
the Son of God, not as we are, by adoption, but by nature; by eternal
filiation, he was the Son of the Highest, "Light of light, very God of
very God", the second Person in the Divine Trinity; and he puts that
Sonship here before God, and says, "Father, Father, forgive them."
Oh, the power of that word from the Son's lip when he is wounded,
when he is in agony, when he is dying! He says, "Father, Father,
grant my one request; O Father, forgive them; for they know not
what they do ;" and the great Father bows his awful head, in token
that the petition is granted.

Then notice, that Jesus here, silently, but really *pleads his sufferings*
The attitude of Christ when he prayed this prayer is very noteworthy.
His hands were stretched upon the transverse beam; his feet were
fastened to the upright tree; and there he pleaded. Silently his
hands and feet were pleading, and his agonized body from every
sinew and muscle pleaded with God. His sacrifice was presented
there before the Father's face; not yet complete, but in his will
complete; and so it is his cross that takes up the plea, "Father, forgive them." O blessed Christ! It is thus that we have been forgiven,
for his Sonship and his cross have pleaded with God, and have
prevailed on our behalf.

I love this prayer, also, because of the *indistinctness* of it. It is
"Father, forgive them." He does not say, "Father, forgive the
soldiers who have nailed me here." He includes them. Neither does
he say, "Father, forgive the people who are beholding me." He
means them. Neither does he say, "Father, forgive sinners in ages
to come who will sin against me." But he means them. Jesus does
not mention them by any accusing name: "Father, forgive my
enemies. Father, forgive my murderers." No, there is no word of
accusation upon those dear lips. "Father, forgive them." Now into
that pronoun "them" I feel that I can crawl. Can you get in there?
Oh, by a humble faith, appropriate the cross of Christ by trusting in
it; and get into that big little word "them"! It seems like a chariot
of mercy that has come down to earth, into which a man may step,
and it shall bear him up to heaven. "Father, forgive them."

Notice, also, what it was that Jesus asked for; to omit that, would
be to leave out the very essence of his prayer. *He asked for full
absolution for his enemies:* "Father, forgive them. Do not punish
them; forgive them. Do not remember their sin; forgive it, blot it
out; throw it into the depths of the sea. Remember it not, my
Father. Mention it not against them any more for ever. Father,
forgive them." Oh, blessed prayer, for the forgiveness of God is
broad and deep! When man forgives, he leaves the remembrance of
the wrong behind; but when God pardons, he says, "I will forgive
their iniquity, and I will remember their sin no more." It is this
that Christ asked for you and me long before we had any repentance,
or any faith; and in answer to that prayer, we were brought to feel
our sin, we were brought to confess it, and to believe in him; and

now, glory be to his name, we can bless him for having pleaded for us, and obtained the forgiveness of all our sins.

IV.   I come now to my last remark, which is this, WE NOW REJOICE IN THE PARDON WE HAVE OBTAINED.

Have you obtained pardon ?   Is this your song ?

> "Now, oh joy ! my sins are pardon'd,
> Now I can, and do believe."

I have a letter, in my pocket, from a man of education and standing, who has been an agnostic; he says that he was a sarcastic agnostic, and he writes praising God, and invoking every blessing upon my head for bringing him to the Saviour's feet.   He says, " I was without happiness for this life, and without hope for the next." I believe that that is a truthful description of many an unbeliever. What hope is there for the world to come apart from the cross of Christ? The best hope such a man has is that he may die the death of a dog, and there may be an end of him.   What is the hope of the Romanist when he comes to die ?   I feel so sorry for many devout and earnest friends, for I do not know what their hope is.   They do not hope to go to heaven yet, at any rate ; some purgatorial pains must be endured first.   Ah, this is a poor, poor faith to die on, to have such a hope as that to trouble your last thoughts.   I do not know of any religion but that of Christ Jesus which tells us of sin pardoned, absolutely pardoned.   Now, listen.   Our teaching is not that, when you come to die, you may, perhaps, find out that it is all right, but, " Beloved, now are we the sons of God."   " He that believeth on the Son hath everlasting life."   He has it now, and he knows it, and he rejoices in it.   So I come back to the last head of my discourse, we rejoice in the pardon Christ has obtained for us.   We are pardoned. I hope that the larger portion of this audience can say, " By the grace of God, we know that we are washed in the blood of the Lamb."

Pardon has come to us through Christ's plea.   Our hope lies in the plea of Christ, and specially in his death. If Jesus paid my debt, and he did if I am a believer in him, then I am out of debt.   If Jesus bore the penalty of my sin, and he did if I am a believer, then there is no penalty for me to pay, for we can say to him,—

> " Complete atonement thou hast made,
> And to the utmost farthing paid
> Whate'er thy people owed :
> Nor can his wrath on me take place,
> If shelter'd in thy righteousness,
> And sprinkled with thy blood.
>
> "If thou hast my discharge procured,
> And freely in my room endured
> The whole of wrath divine:
> Payment God cannot twice demand,
> First at my bleeding Surety's hand,
> And then again at mine."

If Christ has borne my punishment, I shall never bear it.   Oh, what joy there is in this blessed assurance !   Your hope that you are

pardoned lies in this, that Jesus died. Those dear wounds of his
bleed life for you.

We praise him for our pardon because *we do know now what we did.*
Oh, brethren, I know not how much we ought to love Christ, because
we sinned against him so grievously! Now we know that sin is
"exceeding sinful." Now we know that sin crucified Christ. Now
we know that we stabbed our heavenly Lover to his heart. We
slew, with ignominious death, our best and dearest Friend and Benefactor. We know that now; and we could almost weep tears of blood
to think that we ever treated him as we did. But it is all forgiven,
all gone. Oh, let us bless that dear Son of God, who has put away
even such sins as ours! We feel them more now than ever before.
We know they are forgiven, and our grief is because of the pain that
the purchase of our forgiveness cost our Saviour. We never knew
what our sins really were till we saw him in a bloody sweat. We
never knew the crimson hue of our sins till we read our pardon
written in crimson lines with his precious blood. Now, we see our
sin, and yet we do not see it; for God has pardoned it, blotted it
out, cast it behind his back for ever.

Henceforth *ignorance*, such as we have described, *shall be hateful to
us.* Ignorance of Christ and eternal things shall be hateful to us. If,
through ignorance, we have sinned, we will have done with that
ignorance. We will be students of his Word. We will study that
masterpiece of all the sciences, the knowledge of Christ crucified. We
will ask the Holy Ghost to drive far from us the ignorance that
gendereth sin. God grant that we may not fall into sins of ignorance any more; but may we be able to say, "I know whom I have
believed; and henceforth I will seek more knowledge, till I comprehend, with all saints, what are the heights, and depths, and
lengths, and breadths of the love of Christ, and know the love of
God, which passeth knowledge"!

I put in a practical word here. If you rejoice that you are
pardoned, *show your gratitude by your imitation of Christ.* There was
never before such a plea as this, " Father, forgive them; for they know
not what they do." Plead like that for others. Has anybody been
injuring you? Are there persons who slander you? Pray to-night,
" Father, forgive them; for they know not what they do." Let us
always render good for evil, blessing for cursing; and when we are
called to suffer through the wrong-doing of others, let us believe that
they would not act as they do if it were not because of their ignorance. Let us pray for them; and make their very ignorance the
plea for their forgiveness : " Father, forgive them; for they know not
what they do."

I want you also to think of the millions of London just now. See
those miles of streets, pouring out their children this evening; but
look at those public-houses with the crowds streaming in and out.
Go down our streets by moonlight. See what I almost blush to tell.
Follow men and women, too, to their homes, and be this your prayer :
" Father, forgive them; for they know not what they do." That
silver bell—keep it always ringing. What did I say? That silver
bell? Nay, it is the *golden* bell upon the priest's garments. Wear it

on your garments, ye priests of God, and let it always ring out its golden note, "Father, forgive them; for they know not what they do." If I can set all God's saints imitating Christ with such a prayer as this, I shall not have spoken in vain.

Brethren, I see *reason for hope in the very ignorance that surrounds us.* I see hope for this poor city of ours, hope for this poor country, hope for Africa, China, and India. "They know not what they do." Here is a strong argument in their favour, for they are more ignorant than we were. They know less of the evil of sin, and less of the hope of eternal life, than we do. Send up this petition, ye people of God! Heap your prayers together with cumulative power, send up this fiery shaft of prayer, straight to the heart of God, while Jesus from his throne shall add his prevalent intercession, "Father, forgive them; for they know not what they do."

If there be any unconverted people here, and I know that there are some, we will mention them in our private devotion, as well as in the public assembly; and we will pray for them in words like these, "Father, forgive them; for they know not what they do." May God bless you all, for Jesus Christ's sake! Amen.

3. The Believing Thief

"And he said unto Jesus, Lord, remember me when thou comest into thy kingdom. And Jesus said unto him, Verily I say unto thee, To day shalt thou be with me in paradise."—Luke xxiii. 42, 43.

SOME time ago I preached upon the whole story of the dying thief. I do not propose to do the same to-day, but only to look at it from one particular point of view. The story of the salvation of the dying thief is a standing instance of the power of Christ to save, and of his abundant willingness to receive all that come to him, in whatever plight they may be. I cannot regard this act of grace as a solitary instance, any more than the salvation of Zacchæus, the restoration of Peter, or the call of Saul, the persecutor. Every conversion is, in a sense, singular: no two are exactly alike, and yet any one conversion is a type of others. The case of the dying thief is much more similar to our conversion than it is dissimilar; in point of fact, his case may be regarded as typical, rather than as an extraordinary incident. So I shall use it at this time. May the Holy Spirit speak through it to the encouragement of those who are ready to despair!

Remember, beloved friends, that our Lord Jesus, at the time he saved this malefactor, was at his lowest. His glory had been ebbing out in Gethsemane, and before Caiaphas, and Herod, and Pilate; but it had now reached the utmost low-water mark. Stripped of his garments, and nailed to the cross, our Lord was mocked by a ribald crowd, and was dying in agony: then was he "numbered with the transgressors," and made as the offscouring of all things. Yet, while in that condition, he achieved this marvellous deed of grace. Behold the wonder wrought by the Saviour when emptied of all his glory, and hanged up a spectacle of shame upon the brink of death! How certain is it that he can do great wonders of mercy now, seeing that he has returned unto his glory, and sitteth upon the throne of light! "He is able to save them to the uttermost that come unto God by him, seeing he ever liveth to make intercession for them." If a dying Saviour saved the thief, my argument is, that he can do even more now that he liveth and reigneth. All power is given unto him in heaven and in earth; can anything at this present time surpass the power of his grace?

It is not only the weakness of our Lord which makes the salvation of the penitent thief memorable; it is the fact that the dying malefactor saw it before his very eyes. Can you put yourself into his place, and suppose yourself to be looking upon one who hangs in agony upon a cross? Could you readily believe him to be the Lord of glory, who would soon come to his kingdom? That was no mean faith which, at such a moment, could believe in Jesus as Lord and King. If the apostle Paul were here, and wanted to add a New Testament chapter to the eleventh of Hebrews, he might certainly commence his instances of remarkable faith with this thief, who believed in a crucified, derided, and dying Christ, and cried to him as to one whose kingdom would surely come. The thief's faith was the more remarkable because he was himself in great pain, and bound to die. It is not easy to exercise confidence when you are tortured with deadly anguish. Our own rest of mind has at times been greatly hindered by pain of body. When we are the subjects of acute suffering it is not easy to exhibit that faith which we fancy we possess at other times. This man, suffering as he did, and seeing the Saviour in so sad a state, nevertheless believed unto life eternal. Herein was such faith as is seldom seen.

Recollect, also, that he was surrounded by scoffers. It is easy to swim with the current, and hard to go against the stream. This man heard the priests, in their pride, ridicule the Lord, and the great multitude of the common people, with one consent, joined in the scorning; his comrade caught the spirit of the hour, and mocked also, and perhaps he did the same for a while; but through the grace of God he was changed, and believed in the Lord Jesus in the teeth of all the scorn. His faith was not affected by his surroundings; but he, dying thief as he was, made sure his confidence. Like a jutting rock, standing out in the midst of a torrent, he declared the innocence of the Christ whom others blasphemed. His faith is worthy of our imitation in its fruits. He had no member that was free except his tongue, and he used that member wisely to rebuke his brother malefactor, and defend his Lord. His faith brought forth a brave testimony and a bold confession. I am not going to praise the thief, or his faith, but to extol the glory of that grace divine which gave the thief such faith, and then freely saved him by its means. I am anxious to show how glorious is the Saviour—that Saviour to the uttermost, who, at such a time, could save such a man, and give him so great a faith, and so perfectly and speedily prepare him for eternal bliss. Behold the power of that divine Spirit who could produce such faith on soil so unlikely, and in a climate so unpropitious.

Let us enter at once into the centre of our sermon. First, *note the man who was our Lord's last companion on earth;* secondly, *note that this same man was our Lord's first companion at the gate of paradise;* and then, thirdly, let us *note the sermon which our Lord preaches to us from this act of grace.* Oh, for a blessing from the Holy Spirit all the sermon through!

I. Carefully NOTE THAT THE CRUCIFIED THIEF WAS OUR LORD'S LAST

COMPANION ON EARTH. What sorry company our Lord selected when he was here! He did not consort with the religious Pharisees or the philosophic Sadducees, but he was known as "the friend of publicans and sinners." How I rejoice at this! It gives me assurance that he will not refuse to associate with *me*. When the Lord Jesus made a friend of me, he certainly did not make a choice which brought him credit. Do you think he gained any honour when he made a friend of you? Has he ever gained anything by us? No, my brethren; if Jesus had not stooped very low, he would not have come to me; and if he did not seek the most unworthy, he might not have come to you. You feel it so, and you are thankful that he came "not to call the righteous, but sinners to repentance." As the great physician, our Lord was much with the sick: he went where there was room for him to exercise his healing art. The whole have no need of a physician: they cannot appreciate him, nor afford scope for his skill; and therefore he did not frequent their abodes. Yes, after all, our Lord did make a good choice when he saved you and me; for in us he has found abundant room for his mercy and grace. There has been elbow room for his love to work within the awful emptinesses of our necessities and sins; and therein he has done great things for us, whereof we are glad.

Lest any here should be despairing, and say, "He will never deign to look on me," I want you to notice that *the last companion of Christ on earth was a sinner, and no ordinary sinner.* He had broken even the laws of man, for he was a robber. One calls him "a brigand"; and I suppose it is likely to have been the case. The brigands of those days mixed murder with their robberies: he was probably a freebooter in arms against the Roman government, making this a pretext for plundering as he had opportunity. At last he was arrested, and was condemned by a Roman tribunal, which, on the whole, was usually just, and in this case was certainly just; for he himself confesses the justice of his condemnation. The malefactor who believed upon the cross was a convict, who had lain in the condemned cell, and was then undergoing execution for his crimes. A convicted felon was the person with whom our Lord last consorted upon earth. What a lover of the souls of guilty men is he! What a stoop he makes to the very lowest of mankind! To this most unworthy of men the Lord of glory, ere he quitted life, spoke with matchless grace. He spoke to him such wondrous words as never can be excelled if you search the Scriptures through: "To-day shalt thou be with me in paradise." I do not suppose that anywhere in this Tabernacle there will be found a man who has been convicted before the law, or who is even chargeable with a crime against common honesty; but if there should be such a person among my hearers, I would invite him to find pardon and change of heart through our Lord Jesus Christ. You may come to him, whoever you may be; for this man did. Here is a specimen of one who had gone to the extreme of guilt, and who acknowledged that he had done so; he made no excuse, and sought no cloak for his sin; he was in the hands of justice, confronted with the death-doom, and yet he believed in Jesus, and breathed a humble prayer to him, and he was saved upon the spot. As is the sample, such is the bulk. Jesus saves others of like kind. Let me, therefore, put it very plainly here, that none may mistake me. None of you are excluded from the infinite mercy of Christ, however great your iniquity: if you believe in Jesus, he will save *you*.

This man was not only a sinner; *he was a sinner newly awakened*. I do not suppose that he had seriously thought of the Lord Jesus before. According to the other Evangelists, he appears to have joined with his fellow thief in scoffing at Jesus: if he did not actually himself use opprobrious words, he was so far consenting thereunto, that the Evangelist did him no injustice when he said, " The thieves also, which were crucified with him, cast the same in his teeth." Yet, now, on a sudden, he wakes up to the conviction that the man who is dying at his side is something more than a man. He reads the title over his head, and believes it to be true—" This is Jesus the King of the Jews." Thus believing, he makes his appeal to the Messiah, whom he had so newly found, and commits himself to his hands. My hearer, do you see this truth, that the moment a man knows Jesus to be the Christ of God he may at once put his trust in him and be saved? A certain preacher, whose gospel was very doubtful, said, " Do you, who have been living in sin for fifty years, believe that you can in a moment be made clean through the blood of Jesus ? " I answer, " Yes, we do believe that in one moment, through the precious blood of Jesus, the blackest soul can be made white. We do believe that in a single instant the sins of sixty or seventy years can be absolutely forgiven, and that the old nature, which has gone on growing worse and worse, can receive its death-wound in a moment of time, while the life eternal may be implanted in the soul at once." It was so with this man. He had reached the end of his tether, but all of a sudden he woke up to the assured conviction that the Messiah was at his side, and, believing, he looked to him and lived.

So now, my brothers, if you have never in your life before been the subject of any religious conviction, if you have lived up till now an utterly ungodly life, yet if now you will believe that God's dear Son has come into the world to save men from sin, and will unfeignedly confess your sin and trust in him, you shall be immediately saved. Ay, while I speak the word, the deed of grace may be accomplished by that glorious One who has gone up into the heaven with omnipotent power to save.

I desire to put this case very plainly: *this man, who was the last companion of Christ upon earth, was a sinner in misery*. His sins had found him out: he was now enduring the reward of his deeds. I constantly meet with persons in this condition: they have lived a life of wantonness, excess, and carelessness, and they begin to feel the fire-flakes of the tempest of wrath falling upon their flesh ; they dwell in an earthly hell, a prelude of eternal woe. Remorse, like an asp, has stung them, and set their blood on fire: they cannot rest, they are troubled day and night. " Be sure your sin will find you out." It has found them out, and arrested them, and they feel the strong grip of conviction. This man was in that horrible condition: what is more, he was *in extremis*. He could not live long : the crucifixion was sure to be fatal; in a short time his legs would be broken, to end his wretched existence. He, poor soul, had but a short time to live—only the space between noon and sundown; but it was long enough for the Saviour, who is mighty to save. Some are very much afraid that people will put off coming to Christ, if we state this. I cannot help what wicked men do with truth, but I shall state it all the same. If you are now within an hour of death, believe in the Lord Jesus Christ, and you shall be saved. If you never reach your homes again, but drop dead on the road, if you will now believe in the Lord Jesus, you shall be saved: saved now, on the spot. Looking and trusting to Jesus, he will give you a new heart and a right spirit, and blot out your sins. This is the glory of Christ's grace. How I wish I could extol it in proper language! He was last seen on earth before his death in company with a convicted felon, to whom he spoke most lovingly. Come, O ye guilty, and he will receive you graciously!

Once more, *this man whom Christ saved at last was a man who could do no good works.* If salvation had been by good works, he could not have been saved; for he was fastened hand and foot to the tree of doom. It was all over with him as to any act or deed of righteousness. He could say a good word or two, but that was all; he could perform no acts; and if his salvation had depended on an active life of usefulness, certainly he never could have been saved. He was a sinner also, who could not exhibit a long-enduring repentance for sin, for he had so short a time to live. He could not have experienced bitter convictions, lasting over months and years, for his time was measured by moments, and he was on the borders of the grave. His end was very near, and yet the Saviour could save him, and did save him so perfectly, that the sun went not down till he was in paradise with Christ.

This sinner, whom I have painted to you in colours none too black, was *one who believed in Jesus, and confessed his faith.* He did trust the Lord. Jesus was a man, and he called him so; but he knew that he was also Lord, and he called him so, and said, "Lord, remember me." He had such confidence in Jesus, that, if he would but only think of him, if he would only remember him when he came into his kingdom, that would be all that he would ask of him. Alas, my dear hearers! the trouble about some of you is that you know all about my Lord, and yet you do not trust him. Trust is the saving act. Years ago you were on the verge of really trusting Jesus, but you are just as far off from it now as you were then. This man did not hesitate: he grasped the one hope for himself. He did not keep his persuasion of our Lord's Messiahship in his mind as a dry, dead belief, but he turned it into trust and prayer, "Lord, remember me when thou comest into thy kingdom." Oh, that in his infinite mercy many of you would trust my Lord this morning! You shall be saved, I am sure you shall: if you are not saved when you trust, I must myself also renounce all hope. This is all that we have done: we looked, and we lived, and we continue to live because we look to the living Saviour. Oh, that this morning, feeling your sin, you would look to Jesus, trusting him, and confessing that trust! Owning that he is Lord to the glory of God the Father, you must and shall be saved.

In consequence of having this faith which saved him, *this poor man breathed the humble but fitting prayer*, "Lord, remember me." This does not seem to ask much; but as he understood it, it meant all that an anxious heart could desire. As he thought of the kingdom, he had such clear ideas of the glory of the Saviour, that he felt that if the Lord would think of him his eternal state would be safe. Joseph, in prison, asked the chief butler to remember him when he was restored to power; but he forgat him. Our Joseph never forgets a sinner who cried to him in the low dungeon; in his kingdom he remembers the moanings and groanings of poor sinners who are burdened with a sense of sin. Can you not pray this morning, and thus secure a place in the memory of the Lord Jesus?

Thus I have tried to describe the man; and, after having done my best, I shall fail of my object unless I make you see that whatever this thief was, he is a picture of what you are. Especially if you have been a great offender, and if you have been living long without caring for eternal things, you are like that malefactor; and yet you, even you, may do as that thief did; you may believe that Jesus is the Christ, and commit your souls into his hands, and he will save you as surely as he saved the condemned brigand. Jesus graciously says, "Him that cometh to me I will in no wise cast out." This means that if *you* come and trust him, whoever you may be, he will for no reason, and on no ground, and under no circumstances, ever cast you out. Do you catch that thought? Do you feel that it belongs to you, and that if *you* come to him, *you* shall find eternal life? I rejoice if **you so far** perceive the truth.

Few persons have so much intercourse with desponding and despairing souls as I have. Poor cast down ones write to me continually. I scarce know why. I have no special gift of consolation, but I gladly lay myself out to comfort the distressed, and they seem to know it. What joy I have when I see a despairing one find peace! I have had this joy several times during the week just ended. How much I desire that any of you who are breaking your hearts because you cannot find forgiveness would come to my Lord, and trust him, and enter into rest! Has he not said, "Come unto me, all ye that labour and are heavy laden, and I will give you rest"? Come and try him, and that rest shall be yours.

II. In the second place, NOTE, THAT THIS MAN WAS OUR LORD'S COMPANION AT THE GATE OF PARADISE. I am not going into any speculations as to where our Lord went when he quitted the body which hung on the cross. It would seem, from some Scriptures, that he descended into the lower parts of the earth, that he might fill all things. But he very rapidly traversed the regions of the dead. Remember that he died, perhaps an hour or two before the thief, and during that time the eternal glory flamed through the underworld, and was flashing through the gates of paradise just when the pardoned thief was entering the eternal world. Who is this that entereth the pearl-gate at the same moment as the King of glory? Who is this favoured companion of the Redeemer? Is it some honoured martyr? Is it a faithful apostle? Is it a patriarch, like Abraham; or a prince, like David? It is none of these. Behold, and be amazed at sovereign grace. He that goeth in at the gate of paradise, with the King of glory, is a thief, who was saved in the article of death. He is saved in no inferior way, and received into bliss in no secondary style. Verily, there are last which shall be first!

Here I would have you notice *the condescension of our Lord's choice.* The comrade of the Lord of glory, for whom the cherub turns aside his sword of fire, is no great one, but a newly-converted malefactor. And why? I think the Saviour took him with him as a specimen of what he meant to do. He seemed to say to all the heavenly powers, "I bring a sinner with me; he is a sample of the rest." Have you never heard of him who dreamed that he stood without the gate of heaven, and while there he heard sweet music from a band of venerable persons who were on their way to glory? They entered the celestial portals, and there were great rejoicing and shouts. Enquiring "What are these?" he was told that they were the goodly fellowship of the prophets. He sighed, and said, "Alas! I am not one of those." He waited a while, and another band of shining ones drew nigh, who also entered heaven with hallelujahs, and when he enquired, "Who are these, and whence came they?" the answer was, "These are the glorious company of the apostles." Again he sighed, and said, "I cannot enter with them." Then came another body of men white-robed, and bearing palms in their hands, who marched amid great acclamation into the golden city. These he learned were the noble army of martyrs; and again he wept, and said, "I cannot enter with these." In the end he heard the voices of much people, and saw a greater multitude advancing, among whom he perceived Rahab and Mary Magdalene, David and Peter, Manasseh and Saul of Tarsus, and he espied especially the thief, who died at the right hand of Jesus. These all entered in—a strange company. Then he eagerly enquired, "Who are these?" and they answered, "This is the host of sinners saved by grace." Then was he exceeding glad, and said, "I can go with these." Yet, he thought there would be no shouting at the approach of this company, and that they would enter heaven without song; instead of which, there seemed to rise a seven-fold hallelujah of praise unto the Lord of love; for there is joy in the presence of the angels of God over sinners that repent.

I invite any poor soul here that can neither aspire to serve Christ, nor to suffer for him as yet, nevertheless to come in with other believing sinners, in the company of Jesus, who now sets before us an open door.

While we are handling this text, note well *the blessedness of the place* to which the Lord called this penitent. Jesus said, "To day shalt thou be with me in paradise." Paradise means a garden, a garden filled with delights. The garden of Eden is the type of heaven. We know that paradise means heaven, for the apostle speaks of such a man caught up into paradise, and anon he calls it the third heaven. Our Saviour took this dying thief into the paradise of infinite delight, and this is where he will take all of us sinners who believe in him. If we are trusting him, we shall ultimately be with him in paradise.

The next word is better still. Note *the glory of the society* to which this sinner is introduced: "To day shalt thou be **with** *me* **in** paradise." If the Lord said, "To day shalt thou be *with me*," we should not need him to add another word; for where he is, is heaven to us. He added the word "paradise," because else none could have guessed where he was going. Think of it, you uncomely soul; you are to dwell with the Altogether-lovely One for ever. You poor and needy ones, you are to be with him in his glory, in his bliss, in his perfection. Where he is, and as he is, you shall be. The Lord looks into those weeping eyes of yours this morning, and he says, "Poor sinner, thou shalt one day be with me." I think I hear you say, "Lord, that is bliss too great for such a sinner as I am"; but he replies—I have loved thee with an everlasting love: therefore with lovingkindness will I draw thee, till thou shalt be with me where I am.

The stress of the text lies in *the speediness of all this*. "Verily I say unto thee, *To day* shalt thou be with me in paradise." "To day." Thou shalt not lie in purgatory for ages, nor sleep in limbo for so many years; but thou shalt be ready for bliss at once, and at once thou shalt enjoy it. The sinner was hard by the gates of hell, but almighty mercy lifted him up, and the Lord said, "*To day* shalt thou be with me in paradise." What a change from the cross to the crown, from the anguish of Calvary to the glory of the New Jerusalem! In those few hours the beggar was lifted from the dunghill and set among princes. "To day shalt thou be with me in paradise." Can you measure the change from that sinner, loathsome in his iniquity, when the sun was high at noon, to that same sinner, clothed in pure white, and accepted in the Beloved, in the paradise of God, when the sun went down? O glorious Saviour, what marvels thou canst work! How rapidly canst thou work them!

Please notice, also, *the majesty of the Lord's grace* in this text. The Saviour said to him, "Verily *I say* unto thee, To day shalt thou be with me in paradise." Our Lord gives his own will as the reason for saving this man. "I say." He says it who claims the right thus to speak. It is he who will have mercy on whom he will have mercy, and will have compassion on whom he will have compassion. He speaks royally, "Verily I say unto thee." Are they not imperial words? The Lord is a King in whose word there is power. What he says none can gainsay. He that hath the keys of hell and of death saith, "I say unto thee, To day shalt thou be with me in paradise." Who shall prevent the fulfilment of his word?

Notice *the certainty of it*. He says, "Verily." Our blessed Lord on the cross returned to his old majestic manner, as he painfully turned his head, and looked on his convert. He was wont to begin his preaching with, "Verily, verily, I say unto you"; and now that he is dying he uses his favourite manner, and says, "Verily." Our Lord took no oath; his strongest asseveration was, "Verily, verily." To give the penitent the plainest assurance, he says, "Verily I say unto thee, To-day shalt thou be with me in paradise." In this he had an absolutely indisputable assurance that though he must die, yet he would live and find himself in paradise with his Lord.

I have thus shown you that our Lord passed within the pearly gate in company with one to whom he had pledged himself. Why should not you and I pass through that pearl-gate in due time, clothed in his merit, washed in his blood, resting on his power? One of these days angels will say of you, and of me, "Who is this that cometh up from the wilderness, leaning upon her beloved?" The shining ones will be amazed to see some of us coming. If you have lived a life of sin until now, and yet shall repent and enter heaven, what an amazement there will be in every golden street to think that you have come there! In the early Christian church Marcus Caius Victorinus was converted; but he had reached so great an age, and had been so gross a sinner, that the pastor and church doubted him. He gave, however, clear proof of having undergone the divine change, and then there were great acclamations, and many shouts of "Victorinus has become a Christian!" Oh, that some of you big sinners might be saved! How gladly would we rejoice over you! Why not? Would it not glorify God? The salvation of this convicted highwayman has made our Lord illustrious for mercy even unto this day; would not your case do the same? Would not saints cry, "Hallelujah! hallelujah!" if they heard that some of you had been turned from darkness to marvellous light? Why should it not be? Believe in Jesus, and it is so.

III. Now I come to my third and most practical point: NOTE THE LORD'S SERMON TO US FROM ALL THIS.

The devil wants to preach this morning a bit. Yes, Satan asks to come to the front and preach to you; but he cannot be allowed. Avaunt, thou deceiver! Yet I should not wonder if he gets at certain of you when the sermon is over, and whispers, "You see you can be saved at the very last. Put off repentance and faith; you may be forgiven on your death-bed." Sirs, you know who it is that would ruin you by this suggestion. Abhor his deceitful teaching. Do not be ungrateful because God is kind. Do not provoke the Lord because he is patient. Such conduct would be unworthy and ungrateful. Do not run an awful risk because one escaped the tremendous peril. The Lord will accept all who repent; but how do you know that you will repent? It is true that one thief was saved—but the other thief was lost. One is saved, and we may not despair; the other is lost, and we may not presume. Dear friends, I trust you are not made of such diabolical stuff as to fetch from the mercy of God an argument for continuing in sin. If you do, I can only say of you, your damnation will be just; you will have brought it upon yourselves.

Consider now the teaching of our Lord; see *the glory of Christ in salvation.* He is ready to save at the last moment. He was just passing away; his foot was on the doorstep of the Father's house. Up comes this poor sinner the last thing at night, at the eleventh hour, and the Saviour smiles and declares that he will not enter except with this belated wanderer. At the very gate he declares that this seeking soul shall enter with him. There was plenty of time for him to have come before: you know how apt we are to say, "You have waited to the last moment. I am just going off, and I cannot attend to you now." Our Lord had his dying pangs upon him, and yet he attends to the perishing criminal, and permits him to pass through the heavenly portal in his company. Jesus easily saves the sinners for whom he painfully died. Jesus loves to rescue sinners from going down into the pit. You will be very happy if you are saved, but you will not be one half so happy as he will be when he saves you. See how gentle he is!

> " His hand no thunder bears,
>   No terror clothes his brow;
>   No bolts to drive our guilty souls
>   To fiercer flames below."

He comes to us full of tenderness, with tears in his eyes, mercy in his hands, and love in his heart. Believe him to be a great Saviour of great sinners. I have heard of one who had received great mercy who went about saying, " He is a great forgiver; " and I would have you say the same. You shall find your transgressions put away, and your sins pardoned once for all, if you now trust him.

The next doctrine Christ preaches from this wonderful story is *faith in its permitted attachment*. This man believed that Jesus was the Christ. The next thing he did was to appropriate that Christ. He said, " Lord, remember me." Jesus might have said, " What have I to do with you, and what have you to do with me ? What has a thief to do with the perfect One ? " Many of you, good people, try to get as far away as you can from the erring and fallen. They might infect your innocence! Society claims that we should not be familiar with people who have offended against its laws. We must not be seen associating with them, for it might discredit us. Infamous bosh! Can anything discredit sinners such as we are by nature and by practice ? If we know ourselves before God we are degraded enough in and of ourselves ? Is there anybody, after all, in the world, who is worse than we are when we see ourselves in the faithful glass of the Word ? As soon as ever a man believes that Jesus is the Christ, let him hook himself on to him. The moment you believe Jesus to be the Saviour, seize upon him as your Saviour. If I remember rightly, Augustine called this man, *" Latro laudabilis et mirabilis,"* a thief to be praised and wondered at, who dared, as it were, to seize the Saviour for his own. In this he is to be imitated. Take the Lord to be yours, and you have him. Jesus is the common property of all sinners who make bold to take him. Every sinner who has the will to do so may take the Lord home with him. He came into the world to save the sinful. Take him by force, as robbers take their prey; for the kingdom of heaven suffereth the violence of daring faith. Get him, and he will never get himself away from you. If you trust him, he must save you.

Next, notice the doctrine of *faith in its immediate power*.

> " The moment a sinner believes,
>   And trusts in his crucified God,
>   His pardon at once he receives,
>   Redemption in full through his blood."

" To-day shalt thou be with me in paradise." He has no sooner believed than Christ gives him the seal of his believing in the full assurance that he shall be with him for ever in his glory. O dear hearts, if you believe this morning, you shall be saved this morning!

God grant that you, by his rich grace, may be brought into salvation here, on the spot, and at once!

The next thing is, *the nearness of eternal things*. Think of that a minute. Heaven and hell are not places far away. You may be in heaven before the clock ticks again, it is so near. Could we but rend that veil which parts us from the unseen! It is all there, and all near. "To day," said the Lord; within three or four hours at the longest, "shalt thou be with me in paradise;" so near is it. A statesman has given us the expression of being "within measurable distance." We are all within measurable distance of heaven or hell; if there be any difficulty in measuring the distance, it lies in its brevity rather than in its length.

> "One gentle sigh the fetter breaks,
>   We scarce can say, 'He's gone,'
> Before the ransomed spirit takes
>   Its mansion near the throne."

Oh, that we, instead of trifling about such things, because they seem so far away, would solemnly realize them, since they are so very near! This very day, before the sun goes down, some hearer, now sitting in this place, may see, in his own spirit, the realities of heaven or hell. It has frequently happened, in this large congregation, that some one of our audience has died ere the next Sabbath has come round: it may happen this week. Think of that, and let eternal things impress you all the more because they lie so near.

Furthermore, know that *if you have believed in Jesus you are prepared for heaven*. It may be that you will have to live on earth twenty, or thirty, or forty years to glorify Christ; and, if so, be thankful for the privilege; but if you do not live another hour, your instantaneous death would not alter the fact that he that believeth in the Son of God is meet for heaven. Surely, if anything beyond faith is needed to make us fit to enter paradise, the thief would have been kept a little longer here; but no, he is, in the morning, in the state of nature, at noon he enters the state of grace, and by sunset he is in the state of glory. The question never is whether a death-bed repentance is accepted if it be sincere : the question is—Is it sincere ? If it be so, if the man dies five minutes after his first act of faith, he is as safe as if he had served the Lord for fifty years. If your faith is true, if you die one moment after you have believed in Christ, you will be admitted into paradise, even if you shall have enjoyed no time in which to pro- duce good works and other evidences of grace. He that reads the heart will read your faith written on its fleshy tablets, and he will accept you through Jesus Christ, even though no act of grace has been visible to the eye of man.

I conclude by again saying that *this is not an exceptional case.* I began with that, and I want to finish with it, because so many demi- semi-gospellers are so terribly afraid of preaching free grace too fully. I read somewhere, and I think it is true, that some ministers preach the gospel in the same way as donkeys eat thistles, namely, very, very cautiously. On the contrary, I will preach it boldly. I have not the slightest alarm about the matter. If any of you misuse free-grace teaching, I cannot help it. He that will be damned can as well ruin himself by perverting the gospel as by anything else. I cannot help what base hearts may invent; but mine it is to set forth the gospel in all its fulness of grace, and I will do it. If the thief was an exceptional case—and our Lord does not usually act in such a way—there would have been a hint given of so important a fact. A hedge would have been set about this exception to all rules. Would not the Saviour have whispered quietly to the dying man, "You are the only one I am going to treat in this way"? Whenever I have to do an exceptional favour to a person, I have to say, "Do not mention this, or I shall have so many besieging me." If the Saviour had meant this to be a solitary case, he would have faintly said to him, "Do not let anybody know; but you shall to day be in the kingdom with me." No, our Lord spoke openly, and those about him heard what he said. Moreover, the inspired penman has recorded it. If it had been an exceptional case, it would not have been written in the Word of God. Men will not publish their actions in the newspapers if they feel that the record might lead others to expect from them what they cannot give. The Saviour had this wonder of grace reported in the daily news of the gospel, because he means to repeat the marvel every day. The bulk shall be equal to sample, and therefore he sets the sample before you all. He is able to save to the uttermost, for he saved the dying thief. The case would not have been put there to encourage hopes which he cannot fulfil. Whatsoever things were written aforetime were written for our learning, and not for our disappointing. I pray you, therefore, if any of you have not yet trusted in my Lord Jesus, come and trust in him now. Trust him wholly; trust him only; trust him at once. Then will you sing with me—

> " The dying thief rejoiced to see
>   That fountain in his day,
> And there have I, though vile as he,
>   Washed all my sins away."

4. "Lama Sabachthani?"

"And about the ninth hour Jesus cried with a loud voice, saying, Eli, Eli, lama sabachthani? that is to say, My God, my God, why hast thou forsaken me?"—Matthew xxvii. 46.

"THERE was darkness over all the land unto the ninth hour": this cry came out of that darkness. Expect not to see through its every word, as though it came from on high as a beam from the unclouded Sun of Righteousness. There is light in it, bright, flashing light; but there is a centre of impenetrable gloom, where the soul is ready to faint because of the terrible darkness.

Our Lord was then in the darkest part of his way. He had trodden the winepress now for hours, and the work was almost finished. He had reached the culminating point of his anguish. This is his dolorous lament from the lowest pit of misery—"My God, my God, why hast thou forsaken me?" I do not think that the records of time, or even of eternity, contain a sentence more full of anguish. Here the wormwood and the gall, and all the other bitternesses, are outdone. Here you may look as into a vast abyss; and though you strain your eyes, and gaze till sight fails you, yet you perceive no bottom; it is measureless, unfathomable, inconceivable. This anguish of the Saviour on your behalf and mine is no more to be measured and weighed than the sin which needed it, or the love which endured it. We will adore where we cannot comprehend.

I have chosen this subject that it may help the children of God to understand a little of their infinite obligations to their redeeming Lord. You shall measure the height of his love, if it be ever measured, by the depth of his grief, if that can ever be known. See with what a price he hath redeemed us from the curse of the law! As you see this, say to yourselves: What manner of people ought we to be! What measure of love ought we to return to one who bore the utmost penalty, that we might be delivered from the wrath to come? I do not profess that I can dive into this deep: I will only venture to the edge of the precipice, and bid you look down, and pray the Spirit of God to concentrate your mind upon this lamentation of our dying Lord, as it rises up through the thick darkness—"**My God,** my God, why hast thou forsaken me?"

Our first subject of thought will be *the fact;* or, what he suffered— God had forsaken him. Secondly, we will note, *the enquiry;* or, why he suffered: this word "why" is the edge of the text. "Why hast thou forsaken me?" Then, thirdly, we will consider *the answer;* or, what came of his suffering. The answer flowed softly into the soul of the Lord Jesus without the need of words, for he ceased from his anguish with the triumphant shout of, "It is finished." His work was finished, and his bearing of desertion was a chief part of the work he had undertaken for our sake.

I. By the help of the Holy Spirit, let us first dwell upon THE FACT; or, what our Lord suffered. God had forsaken him. Grief of mind is harder to bear than pain of body. You can pluck up courage and endure the pang of sickness and pain, so long as the spirit is hale and brave; but if the soul itself be touched, and the mind becomes diseased with anguish, then every pain is increased in severity, and there is nothing with which to sustain it. Spiritual sorrows are the worst of mental miseries. A man may bear great depression of spirit about worldly matters, if he feels that he has his God to go to. He is cast down, but not in despair. Like David, he dialogues with himself, and he enquires, "Why art thou cast down, O my soul? and why art thou disquieted in me? Hope thou in God: for I shall yet praise him." But if the Lord be once withdrawn, if the comfortable light of his presence be shadowed even for an hour, there is a torment within the breast, which I can only liken to the prelude of hell. This is the greatest of all weights that can press upon the heart. This made the Psalmist plead, "Hide not thy face from me; put not thy servant away in anger." We can bear a bleeding body, and even a wounded spirit; but a soul conscious of desertion by God is beyond conception unendurable. When he holdeth back the face of his throne, and spreadeth his cloud upon it, who can endure the darkness?

This voice out of "the belly of hell" marks the lowest depth of the Saviour's grief. *The desertion was real.* Though under some aspects our Lord could say, "The Father is with me"; yet was it solemnly true that God did forsake him. It was not a failure of faith on his part which led him to imagine what was not actual fact. Our faith fails us, and then we think that God has forsaken us; but our Lord's faith did not for a moment falter, for he says twice, "*My* God, *my* God." Oh, the mighty double grip of his unhesitating faith! He seems to say, "Even if thou hast forsaken me, I have not forsaken thee." Faith triumphs, and there is no sign of any faintness of heart towards the living God. Yet, strong as is his faith, he feels that God has withdrawn his comfortable fellowship, and he shivers under the terrible deprivation.

It was no fancy, or delirium of mind, caused by his weakness of body, the heat of the fever, the depression of his spirit, or the near approach of death. He was clear of mind even to this last. He bore up under pain, loss of blood, scorn, thirst, and desolation; making no complaint of the cross, the nails, and the scoffing. We read not in the Gospels of anything more than the natural cry of weakness, "I thirst." All the tortures of his body he endured in silence; but when it came to being forsaken of God, then his great heart burst out into its "Lama sabachthani?" His one moan is concerning his God. It is not, "Why has Peter forsaken me? Why has Judas betrayed me?" These were sharp griefs, but this is the sharpest. This stroke has cut him to the quick: "My God, my God, why hast *thou* forsaken me?" It was no phantom of the gloom; it was a real absence which he mourned.

This was *a very remarkable desertion.* It is not the way of God to leave either his sons or his servants. His saints, when they come to die, in their great weakness and pain, find him near. They are made to sing because of the presence of God: "Yea, though I walk through the valley of the shadow of death, I will fear no evil: for thou art with me." Dying saints have clear visions of the living God. Our observation has taught us that if the Lord be away at other times, he is never absent from his people in the article of death, or in the furnace of affliction. Concerning the three holy children, we do not read that the Lord was ever visibly with them till they walked the fires of Nebuchadnezzar's furnace; but there and then the Lord met with them. Yes, beloved, it is God's use and wont to keep company with his afflicted people; and yet he forsook his Son in the hour of his tribulation! How usual it is to see the Lord with his faithful witnesses when resisting even unto blood! Read the Book of Martyrs, and I care not whether you study the former or the later persecutions, you will find them all lit up with the evident presence of the Lord with his witnesses. Did the Lord ever fail to support a martyr at the stake? Did he ever forsake one of his testifiers upon the scaffold? The testimony of the church has always been, that while the Lord has permitted his saints to suffer in body he has so divinely sustained their spirits that they have been more than conquerors, and have treated their sufferings as light afflictions. The fire has not been a "bed of roses," but it has been a chariot of victory. The sword is sharp, and death is bitter; but the love of Christ is sweet, and to die for him has been turned into glory. No, it is not God's way to forsake his champions, nor to leave even the least of his children in the trial hour.

As to our Lord, this forsaking was *singular.* Did his Father ever leave him before? Will you read the four Evangelists through and find any previous instance in which he complains of his Father for having forsaken him? No. He said, "I know that thou hearest me always." He lived in constant touch with God. His fellowship with the Father was always near and dear and clear; but now, for the first time, he cries, "why hast thou forsaken me?" It was very remarkable. It was a riddle only to be solved by the fact that he loved us and gave himself for us, and in the execution of his loving purpose came even unto this sorrow, of mourning the absence of his God.

This forsaking was *very terrible.* Who can fully tell what it is to be forsaken of God? We can only form a guess by what we have ourselves felt under temporary and partial desertion. God has never left us, altogether; for he has expressly said, "I will never leave thee, nor forsake thee"; yet we have sometimes felt as if he had cast us off. We have cried, "Oh, that I knew where I might find him!" The clear shinings of his love have been withdrawn. Thus we are able to form some little idea of how the Saviour felt when his God had forsaken him. The mind of Jesus was left to dwell upon one dark subject, and no cheering theme consoled him. It was the hour in which he was made to stand before God as consciously the sin-bearer, according to that ancient prophecy, "He shall bear their iniquities." Then was it true, "He hath made him to be sin for us." Peter puts it, "He his own self bare our sins in his own body on the tree." Sin, sin, sin was everywhere around and about Christ. He had no sin of his own; but the Lord had "laid on him the iniquity of us all." He had no strength given him from on high, no secret oil and wine poured into his wounds; but he was made to appear in the lone character of the Lamb of God, which taketh away the sin of the world; and therefore he must feel the weight of sin, and the turning away of that sacred face which cannot look thereon.

His Father, at that time, gave him no open acknowledgment. On certain other occasions a voice had been heard, saying, "This is my beloved Son, in whom I am well pleased"; but now, when such a testimony seemed most of all required, the oracle was dumb. He was hung up as an accursed thing upon the cross; for he was "made a curse for us, as it is written, Cursed is every one that hangeth on a tree"; and the Lord his God did not own him before men. If it had pleased the Father, he might have sent him twelve legions of angels; but not an angel came after the Christ had quitted Gethsemane. His despisers might spit in his face, but no swift seraph came to avenge the indignity. They might bind him, and scourge him, but none of all the heavenly host would interpose to screen his shoulders from the lash. They might fasten him to the tree with nails, and lift him up, and scoff at him; but no cohort of ministering spirits hastened to drive back the rabble, and release the Prince of life. No, he appeared to be forsaken, "smitten of God and afflicted," delivered into the hands of cruel men, whose wicked hands worked him misery without stint. Well might he ask, "My God, my God, why hast thou forsaken me?"

But this was not all. His Father now dried up that sacred stream of peaceful communion and loving fellowship which had flowed hitherto throughout his whole earthly life. He said himself, as you remember, "Ye shall be scattered, every man to his own, and shall leave me alone: and yet I am not alone, because the Father is with me." Here was his constant comfort: but all comfort from this source was to be withdrawn. The divine Spirit did not minister to his human spirit. No communications with his Father's love poured into his heart. It was not possible that the Judge should smile upon one who represented the prisoner at the bar. Our Lord's faith did not fail him, as I have already shown you, for he said, "My God, my God": yet no sensible supports were given to his heart, and no comforts were poured into his mind. One writer declares that Jesus did not taste of divine wrath, but only suffered a withdrawal of divine fellowship. What is the difference? Whether God withdraw heat or create cold is all one. He was not smiled upon, nor allowed to feel that he was near to God; and this, to his tender spirit, was grief of the keenest order. A certain saint once said that in his sorrow he had from God "necessaries, but not suavities"; that which was meet, but not that which was sweet. Our Lord suffered to the extreme point of deprivation. He had not the light which makes existence to be life, and life to be a boon. You that know, in your degree, what it is to lose the conscious presence and love of God, you can faintly guess what the sorrow of the Saviour was, now that he felt he had been forsaken of his God. "If the foundations be removed, what can the righteous do?" To our Lord, the Father's love was the foundation of everything; and when that was gone, all was gone. Nothing remained, within, without, above, when his own God, the God of his entire confidence, turned from him. Yes, God in very deed forsook our Saviour.

To be forsaken of God was *much more a source of anguish to Jesus than it would be to us.* "Oh," say you, "how is that?" I answer, because he was perfectly holy. A rupture between a perfectly holy being and the thrice holy God must be in the highest degree strange, abnormal, perplexing, and painful. If any man here, who is not at peace with God, could only know his true condition, he would swoon with fright. If you unforgiven ones only knew where you are, and what you are at this moment in the sight of God, you would never smile again till you were reconciled to him. Alas! we are insensible, hardened by the deceitfulness of sin, and therefore we do not feel our true condition. His perfect holiness made it to our Lord a dreadful calamity to be forsaken of the thrice holy God.

I remember, also, that our blessed Lord had lived in unbroken fellowship with God, and to be forsaken was a new grief to him. He had never known what the dark was till then: his life had been lived in the light of God. Think, dear child of God, if you had always dwelt in full communion with God, your days would have been as the days of heaven upon earth; and how cold it would strike to your heart to find yourself in the darkness of desertion. If you can conceive such a thing as happening to a perfect man, you can see why to our Well-beloved it was a special trial. Remember, he had enjoyed fellowship with God more richly, as well as more constantly, than any of us. His fellowship with the Father was of the highest, deepest, fullest order; and what must the loss of it have been? We lose but drops when we lose our joyful experience of heavenly fellowship; and yet the loss is killing: but to our Lord Jesus Christ the sea was dried up—I mean his sea of fellowship with the infinite God.

Do not forget that he was such a One that to him to be without God must have been an overwhelming calamity. In every part he was perfect, and in every part fitted for communion with God to a supreme degree. A sinful man has an awful need of God, but he does not know it; and therefore he does not feel that hunger and thirst after God which would come upon a perfect man could he be deprived of God. The very perfection of his nature renders it inevitable that the holy man must either be in communion with God, or be desolate. Imagine a stray angel! a seraph who has lost his God! Conceive him to be perfect in holiness, and yet to have fallen into a condition in

which he cannot find his God! I cannot picture him; perhaps a
Milton might have done so. He is sinless and trustful, and yet he
has an overpowering feeling that God is absent from him. He has
drifted into the nowhere—the unimaginable region behind the back
of God. I think I hear the wailing of the cherub: "My God, my
God, my God, where art thou?" What a sorrow for one of the sons
of the morning! But here we have the lament of a Being far more
capable of fellowship with the Godhead. In proportion as he is more
fitted to receive the love of the great Father, in that proportion is his
pining after it the more intense. As a Son, he is more able to commune
with God than ever a servant-angel could be; and now that he is
forsaken of God, the void within is the greater, and the anguish
more bitter.

Our Lord's heart, and all his nature were, morally and spiritually,
so delicately formed, so sensitive, so tender, that to be without God,
was to him a grief which could not be weighed. I see him in the
text bearing desertion, and yet I perceive that he cannot bear it. I
know not how to express my meaning except by such a paradox. He
cannot endure to be without God. He had surrendered himself to be
left of God, as the representative of sinners must be, but his pure and
holy nature, after three hours of silence, finds the position unendurable
to love and purity; and breaking forth from it, now that the hour was
over, he exclaims, "Why hast thou forsaken me?" He quarrels not
with the suffering, but he cannot abide in the position which caused it.
He seems as if he must end the ordeal, not because of the pain, but
because of the moral shock. We have here the repetition after his
passion of that loathing which he felt before it, when he cried, "If it
be possible let this cup pass from me: nevertheless not as I will, but as
thou wilt." "My God, my God, why hast thou forsaken me?" is the
holiness of Christ amazed at the position of substitute for guilty men.

There, friends; I have done my best, but I seem to myself to have
been prattling like a little child, talking about something infinitely
above me. So I leave the solemn fact, that our Lord Jesus was on the
tree forsaken of his God.

II. This brings us to consider THE ENQUIRY, or, why he suffered.

Note carefully this cry—"My God, my God, why hast thou forsaken
me?" It is pure anguish, undiluted agony, which crieth like this;
but it is the agony of a godly soul; for only a man of that order would
have used such an expression. Let us learn from it useful lessons.
This cry is taken from "the Book." Does it not show our Lord's love
of the sacred volume, that when he felt his sharpest grief, he turned
to the Scripture to find a fit utterance for it? Here we have the
opening sentence of the twenty-second Psalm. Oh, that we may so
love the inspired Word that we may not only sing to its score, but
even weep to its music!

Note, again, that our Lord's lament is an address to God. The
godly, in their anguish, turn to the hand which smites them. The
Saviour's outcry is not *against* God, but *to* God. "My God, my God":
he makes a double effort to draw near. True Sonship is here. The
child in the dark is crying after his Father—"My God, my God."
Both the Bible and prayer were dear to Jesus in his agony.

Still, observe, it is a faith-cry; for though it asks, "Why hast thou forsaken me?" yet it first says, twice over, "My God, my God." The grip of appropriation is in the word "my"; but the reverence of humility is in the word "God." It is "'My *God*, my *God*,' thou art ever God to me, and I a poor creature. I do not quarrel with thee. Thy rights are unquestioned, for thou art my *God*. Thou canst do as thou wilt, and I yield to thy sacred sovereignty. I kiss the hand that smites me, and with all my heart I cry, 'My God, my God.'" When you are delirious with pain, think of your Bible still : when your mind wanders, let it roam towards the mercy seat ; and when your heart and your flesh fail, still live by faith, and still cry, "My God, my God."

Let us come close to the enquiry. It looked to me, at first sight, like *a question as of one distraught,* driven from the balance of his mind— not unreasonable, but too much reasoning, and therefore tossed about. "Why hast thou forsaken me?" Did not Jesus know ? Did he not know why he was forsaken ? He knew it most distinctly, and yet his manhood, while it was being crushed, pounded, dissolved, seemed as though it could not understand the reason for so great a grief. He must be forsaken ; but could there be a sufficient cause for so sickening a sorrow ? The cup must be bitter ; but why this most nauseous of ingredients ? I tremble lest I say what I ought not to say. I have said it, and I think there is truth—the Man of Sorrows was overborne with horror. At that moment the finite soul of the man Christ Jesus came into awful contact with the infinite justice of God. The one Mediator between God and man, the man Christ Jesus, beheld the holiness of God in arms against the sin of man, whose nature he had espoused. God was for him and with him in a certain unquestionable sense ; but for the time, so far as his feeling went, God was against him, and necessarily withdrawn from him. It is not surprising that the holy soul of Christ should shudder at finding itself brought into painful contact with the infinite justice of God, even though its design was only to vindicate that justice, and glorify the Law-giver. Our Lord could now say, "All thy waves and thy billows are gone over me"; and therefore he uses language which is all too hot with anguish to be dissected by the cold hand of a logical criticism. Grief has small regard for the laws of the grammarian. Even the holiest, when in extreme agony, though they cannot speak otherwise than according to purity and truth, yet use a language of their own, which only the ear of sympathy can fully receive. I see not all that is here, but what I can see I am not able to put in words for you.

I think I see, in the expression, submission and resolve. Our Lord does not draw back. There is a forward movement in the question : they who quit a business ask no more questions about it. He does not ask that the forsaking may end prematurely, he would only understand anew its meaning. He does not shrink, but the rather dedicates himself anew to God by the words, "My God, my God," and by seeking to review the ground and reason of that anguish which he is resolute to bear even to the bitter end. He would fain feel anew the motive which has sustained him, and must sustain him to the end. The cry sounds to me like deep submission and strong resolve, pleading with God.

Do you not think that *the amazement of our Lord, when he was "made sin for us"* (2 Cor. v. 21), led him thus to cry out? For such a sacred and pure being to be made a sin-offering was an amazing experience. Sin was laid on him, and he was treated as if he had been guilty, though he had personally never sinned; and now the infinite horror of rebellion against the most holy God fills his holy soul, the unrighteousness of sin breaks his heart, and he starts back from it, crying, "My God, my God, why hast thou forsaken *me?*" Why must I bear the dread result of conduct I so much abhor?

Do you not see, moreover, *there was here a glance at his eternal purpose, and at his secret source of joy?* That "why" is the silver lining of the dark cloud, and our Lord looked wishfully at it. He knew that the desertion was needful in order that he might save the guilty, and he had an eye to that salvation as his comfort. He is not forsaken needlessly, nor without a worthy design. The design is in itself so dear to his heart that he yields to the passing evil, even though that evil be like death to him. He looks at that "why," and through that narrow window the light of heaven comes streaming into his darkened life.

"My God, my God, why hast thou forsaken me?" Surely our Lord dwelt on that "why," *that we might also turn our eyes that way.* He would have us see the why and the wherefore of his grief. He would have us mark the gracious motive for its endurance. Think much of all your Lord suffered, but do not overlook the reason of it. If you cannot always understand how this or that grief worked toward the great end of the whole passion, yet believe that it has its share in the grand "why." Make a life-study of that bitter but blessed question, "Why hast thou forsaken me?" Thus the Saviour raises an inquiry not so much for himself as for us; and not so much because of any despair within his heart as because of a hope and a joy set before him, which were wells of comfort to him in his wilderness of woe.

Bethink you, for a moment, that the Lord God, in the broadest and most unreserved sense, could never, in very deed, have forsaken his most obedient Son. He was ever with him in the grand design of salvation. Towards the Lord Jesus, personally, God himself, personally, must ever have stood on terms of infinite love. Truly the Only Begotten was never more lovely to the Father than when he was obedient unto death, even the death of the cross! But we must look upon God here as the Judge of all the earth, and we must look upon the Lord Jesus also in his official capacity, as the Surety of the covenant, and the Sacrifice for sin. The great Judge of all cannot smile upon him who has become the substitute for the guilty. Sin is loathed of God; and if, in order to its removal, his own Son is made to bear it, yet, as sin, it is still loathsome, and he who bears it cannot be in happy communion with God. This was the dread necessity of expiation; but in the essence of things the love of the great Father to his Son never ceased, nor ever knew a diminution. Restrained in its flow it must be, but lessened at its fountain-head it could not be. Therefore, wonder not at the question, "Why hast thou forsaken me?"

III Hoping to be guided by the Holy Spirit, I am coming to

THE ANSWER, concerning which I can only use the few minutes which remain to me. "My God, my God, why hast thou forsaken me?" What is the outcome of this suffering? What was the reason for it? Our Saviour could answer his own question. If for a moment his manhood was perplexed, yet his mind soon came to clear apprehension; for he said, "It is finished"; and, as I have already said, he then referred to the work which in his lonely agony he had been performing. Why, then, did God forsake his Son? I cannot conceive any other answer than this—*he stood in our stead.* There was no reason in Christ why the Father should forsake him: he was perfect, and his life was without spot. God never acts without reason; and since there were no reasons in the character and person of the Lord Jesus why his Father should forsake him, we must look elsewhere. I do not know how others answer the question. I can only answer it in this one way.

> " Yet all the griefs he felt were ours,
> Ours were the woes he bore;
> Pangs, not his own, his spotless soul
> With bitter anguish tore.

> " We held him as condemn'd of heaven,
> An outcast from his God;
> While for our sins he groaned, he bled,
> Beneath his Father's rod."

He bore the sinner's sin, and he had to be treated, therefore, as though he were a sinner, though sinner he could never be. With his own full consent he suffered as though he had committed the transgressions which were laid on him. Our sin, and his taking it upon himself, is the answer to the question, "Why hast thou forsaken me?"

In this case we now see that *His obedience was perfect.* He came into the world to obey the Father, and he rendered that obedience to the very uttermost. The spirit of obedience could go no farther than for one who feels forsaken of God still to cling to him in solemn, avowed allegiance, still declaring before a mocking multitude his confidence in the afflicting God. It is noble to cry, "My God, my God," when one is asking, "Why hast thou forsaken me?" How much farther can obedience go? I see nothing beyond it. The soldier at the gate of Pompeii remaining at his post as sentry when the shower of burning ashes is falling, was not more true to his trust than he who adheres to a forsaking God with loyalty of hope.

Our Lord's suffering in this particular form was appropriate and necessary. It would not have sufficed for our Lord merely to have been pained in body, nor even to have been grieved in mind in other ways: he must suffer in this particular way. He must feel forsaken of God, because this is the necessary consequence of sin. For a man to be forsaken of God is the penalty which naturally and inevitably follows upon his breaking his relation with God. What is death? What was the death that was threatened to Adam? "In the day that thou eatest thereof thou shalt surely die." Is death annihilation? Was Adam annihilated that day? Assuredly not: he lived many a year afterwards. But in the day in which he ate of the forbidden fruit he died, by being separated from God. The separation of the soul from God is spiritual death ; just as the separation of the soul from the body is natural death. The sacrifice for sin must be put in the place of separation, and must bow to the penalty of death. By this placing of the Great Sacrifice under forsaking and death, it would be seen by all creatures throughout the universe that God could not have fellowship with sin. If even the Holy One, who stood the Just for the unjust, found God forsaking him, what must the doom of the actual sinner be! Sin is evidently always, in every case, a dividing influence, putting even the Christ himself, as a sin-bearer, in the place of distance.

This was necessary for another reason : there could have been no laying on of suffering for sin without the forsaking of the vicarious Sacrifice by the Lord God. So long as the smile of God rests on the man the law is not afflicting him. The approving look of the great Judge cannot fall upon a man who is viewed as standing in the place of the guilty. Christ not only suffered *from* sin, but *for* sin. If God will cheer and sustain him, he is not suffering for sin. The Judge is not inflicting suffering for sin if he is manifestly succouring the smitten one. There could have been no vicarious suffering on the part of Christ for human guilt, if he had continued consciously to enjoy the full sunshine of the Father's presence. It was essential to being a victim in our place that he should cry, " My God, my God, why hast thou forsaken me ? "

Beloved, see how marvellously, in the person of Christ, the Lord our God has vindicated his law ! If to make his law glorious, he had said, "These multitudes of men have broken my law, and therefore they shall perish," the law would have been terribly magnified. But, instead thereof, he says, " Here is my Only Begotten Son, my other self; he takes on himself the nature of these rebellious creatures, and he consents that I should lay on him the load of their iniquity, and visit in his person the offences which might have been punished in the persons of all these multitudes of men : and I will have it so." When Jesus bows his head to the stroke of the law, when he sub-missively consents that his Father shall turn away his face from him, then myriads of worlds are astonished at the perfect holiness and stern justice of the Lawgiver. There are, probably, worlds innumerable throughout the boundless creation of God, and all these will see, in the death of God's dear Son, a declaration of his determination never to allow sin to be trifled with. If his own Son is brought before him, bearing the sin of others upon him, he will hide his face from him, as well as from the actually guilty. In God infinite love shines over all, but it does not eclipse his absolute justice any more than his justice is permitted to destroy his love. God hath all perfections in perfection, and in Christ Jesus we see the reflection of them. Beloved, this is a wonderful theme ! Oh, that I had a tongue worthy of this subject ! but who could ever reach the height of this great argument ?

Once more, when enquiring, Why did Jesus suffer to be forsaken of the Father ? we see the fact that *the Captain of our salvation was thus made perfect through suffering.* Every part of the road has been traversed by our Lord's own feet. Suppose, beloved, the Lord Jesus had never been thus forsaken, then one of his disciples might have been called to that sharp endurance, and the Lord Jesus could not have sympathized with him in it. He would turn to his Leader and Captain, and say to him, "Didst thou, my Lord, ever feel this darkness?" Then the Lord Jesus would answer, "No. This is a descent such as I never made." What a dreadful lack would the tried one have felt! For the servant to bear a grief his Master never knew would be sad indeed.

There would have been a wound for which there was no ointment, a pain for which there was no balm. But it is not so now. "In all their affliction he was afflicted." "He was in all points tempted like as we are, yet without sin." Wherein we greatly rejoice at this time, and so often as we are cast down. Underneath us is the deep experience of our forsaken Lord.

I have done when I have said three things. The first is, you and I that are believers in the Lord Jesus Christ, and are resting in him alone for salvation, *let us lean hard*, let us bear with all our weight on our Lord. He will bear the full weight of all our sin and care. As to my sin, I hear its harsh accusings no more when I hear Jesus cry, "Why hast thou forsaken me?" I know that I deserve the deepest hell at the hand of God's vengeance; but I am not afraid. He will never forsake *me*, for he forsook his Son on my behalf. I shall not suffer for my sin, for Jesus has suffered to the full in my stead; yea, suffered so far as to cry, "My God, my God, why hast thou forsaken me?" Behind this brazen wall of substitution a sinner is safe. These "munitions of rock" guard all believers, and they may rest secure. The rock is cleft for me; I hide in its rifts, and no harm can reach me. You have a full atonement, a great sacrifice, a glorious vindication of the law; wherefore rest at peace, all you that put your trust in Jesus.

Next, if ever in our lives henceforth we should think that God hath deserted us, *let us learn from our Lord's example how to behave ourselves.* If God hath left thee, do not shut up thy Bible; nay, open it, as thy Lord did, and find a text that will suit thee. If God hath left thee, or thou thinkest so, do not give up prayer; nay, pray as thy Lord did, and be more earnest than ever. If thou thinkest God has forsaken thee, do not give up thy faith in him; but, like thy Lord, cry thou, "My God, my God," again and again. If thou hast had one anchor before, cast out two anchors now, and double the hold of thy faith. If thou canst not call Jehovah "Father," as was Christ's wont, yet call him thy "God." Let the personal pronouns take their hold—"My God, my God." Let nothing drive thee from thy faith. Still hold on Jesus, sink or swim. As for me, if ever I am lost, it shall be at the foot of the cross. To this pass have I come, that if I never see the face of God with acceptance, yet I will believe that he will be faithful to his Son, and true to the covenant sealed by oaths and blood. He that believeth in Jesus hath everlasting life: there I cling, like the limpet to the rock. There is but one gate of heaven, and even if I may not enter it, I will cling to the posts of its door. What am I saying? I shall enter in; for that gate was never shut against a soul that accepted Jesus; and Jesus saith, "Him that cometh to me I will in no wise cast out."

The last of the three points is this, *let us abhor the sin which brought such agony upon our beloved Lord.* What an accursed thing is sin, which crucified the Lord Jesus! Do you laugh at it? Will you go and spend an evening to see a mimic performance of it? Do you roll sin under your tongue as a sweet morsel, and then come to God's house, on the Lord's-day morning, and think to worship him? Worship him! Worship him, with sin indulged in your breast! Worship him, with sin loved and pampered in your life! O sirs, if I had a dear brother who had been murdered, what would you think of me if I valued the knife which had been crimsoned with his blood? —if I made a friend of the murderer, and daily consorted with the assassin, who drove the dagger into my brother's heart? Surely I, too, must be an accomplice in the crime! Sin murdered Christ; will you be a friend to it? Sin pierced the heart of the Incarnate God; can you love it? Oh, that there was an abyss as deep as Christ's misery, that I might at once hurl this dagger of sin into its depths, whence it might never be brought to light again! Begone, O sin! Thou art banished from the heart where Jesus reigns! Begone, for thou hast crucified my Lord, and made him cry, "Why hast thou forsaken me?" O my hearers, if you did but know yourselves, and know the love of Christ, you would each one vow that you would harbour sin no longer. You would be indignant at sin, and cry,

> "The dearest idol I have known,
>   Whate'er that idol be,
> Lord, I will tear it from its throne,
>   And worship only thee."

May that be the issue of my morning's discourse, and then I shall be well content. The Lord bless you! May the Christ who suffered for you, bless you, and out of his darkness may your light arise! Amen.

5. The Shortest
of the Seven Cries

"After this, Jesus knowing that all things were now accomplished, that the scripture might be fulfilled, saith, I thirst."—John xix. 28.

It was most fitting that every word of our Lord upon the cross should be gathered up and preserved. As not a bone of him shall be broken, so not a word shall be lost. The Holy Spirit took special care that each of the sacred utterances should be fittingly recorded. There were, as you know, seven of those last words, and seven is the number of perfection and fulness ; the number which blends the three of the infinite God with the four of complete creation. Our Lord in his death-cries, as in all else, was perfection itself. There is a fulness of meaning in each utterance which no man shall be able fully to bring forth, and when combined they make up a vast deep of thought, which no human line can fathom. Here, as everywhere else, we are constrained to say of our Lord, " Never man spake like this man." Amid all the anguish of his spirit his last words prove him to have remained fully self-possessed, true to his forgiving nature, true to his kingly office, true to his filial relationship, true to his God, true to his love of the written word, true to his glorious work, and true to his faith in his Father.

As these seven sayings were so faithfully recorded, we do not wonder that they have frequently been the subject of devout meditation. Fathers and confessors, preachers and divines have delighted to dwell upon every syllable of these matchless cries. These solemn sentences have shone like the seven golden candlesticks or the seven stars of the Apocalypse, and have lighted multitudes of men to him who spake them. Thoughtful men have drawn a wealth of meaning from them, and in so doing have arranged them into different groups, and placed them under several heads. I cannot give you more than a mere taste of this rich subject, but I have been most struck with two ways of regarding our Lord's last words. First, they teach and confirm many of the doctrines of our holy faith. " *Father, forgive them ; for they know not what they do* " is the first. Here is the forgiveness of sin—free forgiveness in answer to the

Saviour's plea. "*To-day shalt thou be with me in paradise.*" Here is the safety of the believer in the hour of his departure, and his instant admission into the presence of his Lord. It is a blow at the fable of purgatory which strikes it to the heart. "*Woman, behold thy son!*" This very plainly sets forth the true and proper humanity of Christ, who to the end recognised his human relationship to Mary, of whom he was born. Yet his language teaches us not to worship *her*, for he calls her "woman," but to honour him who in his direst agony thought of her needs and griefs, as he also thinks of all his people, for these are his mother and sister and brother. "*Eloi, Eloi, lama sabachthani?*" is the fourth cry, and it illustrates the penalty endured by our Substitute when he bore our sins, and so was forsaken of his God. The sharpness of that sentence no exposition can fully disclose to us : it is keen as the very edge and point of the sword which pierced his heart. "*I thirst*" is the fifth cry, and its utterance teaches us the truth of Scripture, for all things were accomplished, that the Scripture might be fulfilled, and therefore our Lord said, "I thirst." Holy Scripture remains the basis of our faith, established by every word and act of our Redeemer. The last word but one is, "*It is finished.*" There is the complete justification of the believer, since the work by which he is accepted is fully accomplished. The last of his last words is also taken from the Scriptures, and shows where his mind was feeding. He cried, ere he bowed the head which he had held erect amid all his conflict, as one who never yielded, "*Father, into thy hands I commend my spirit.*" In that cry there is reconciliation to God. He who stood in our stead has finished all his work, and now his spirit comes back to the Father, and he brings us with him. Every word, therefore, you see teaches us some grand fundamental doctrine of our blessed faith. "He that hath ears to hear, let him hear."

A second mode of treating these seven cries is to view them as setting forth the person and offices of our Lord who uttered them. "*Father, forgive them ; for they know not what they do*"—here we see the Mediator interceding : Jesus standing before the Father pleading for the guilty. "*Verily I say unto thee, to-day shalt thou be with me in paradise*"—this is the Lord Jesus in kingly power, opening with the key of David a door which none can shut, admitting into the gates of heaven the poor soul who had confessed him on the tree. Hail, everlasting King in heaven, thou dost admit to thy paradise whomsoever thou wilt! Nor dost thou set a time for waiting, but instantly thou dost set wide the gate of pearl; thou hast all power in heaven as well as upon earth. Then came, "*Woman, behold thy son!*" wherein we see the Son of man in the gentleness of a son caring for his bereaved mother. In the former cry, as he opened Paradise, you saw the Son of God; now you see him who was verily and truly born of a woman, made under the law; and under the law you see him still, for he honours his mother and cares for her in the last article of death. Then comes the "*My God, my God, why hast thou forsaken me ?*" Here we behold his human *soul* in anguish, his inmost heart overwhelmed by the withdrawing of Jehovah's face, and made to cry out as if in perplexity and amazement. "*I thirst,*" is his human *body* tormented by grievous pain. Here you see how the mortal flesh had to share in the agony of the inward spirit. "*It is finished*" is the last word but one, and there you see the perfected Saviour, the Captain of our salvation, who has completed the undertaking upon which he had entered, finished transgression, made an end of sin, and brought in everlasting righteousness. The last expiring word in which he *commended his spirit to his Father*, is the note of acceptance for himself and for us all. As he commends his spirit into the Father's hand, so does he bring all believers nigh to God, and henceforth we are in the hand of the Father, who is greater than all, and none shall pluck us thence. Is not this a fertile field of thought? May the Holy Spirit often lead us to glean therein.

There are many other ways in which these words might be read, and they would be found to be all full of instruction. Like the steps of a ladder or the links of a golden chain, there is a mutual dependence and interlinking of each of the cries, so that one leads to another and that to a third. Separately or in connection our Master's words overflow with instruction to thoughtful minds: but of all save one I must say, " Of which we cannot now speak particularly."

Our text is the shortest of all the words of Calvary ; it stands as two words in our language—" I thirst," but in the Greek it is only one. I cannot say that it is short and sweet, for, alas, it was bitterness itself to our Lord Jesus ; and yet out of its bitterness I trust there will come great sweetness to us. Though bitter to him in the speaking it will be sweet to us in the hearing,—so sweet that all the bitterness of our trials shall be forgotten as we remember the vinegar and gall of which he drank.

We shall by the assistance of the Holy Spirit try to regard these words of our Saviour in a five-fold light. First, we shall look upon them as THE ENSIGN OF HIS TRUE HUMANITY. Jesus said, " I thirst," and this is the complaint of a man. Our Lord is the Maker of the ocean and the waters that are above the firmament : it is his hand that stays or opens the bottles of heaven, and sendeth rain upon the evil and upon the good. " The sea is his, and he made it," and all fountains and springs are of his digging. He poureth out the streams that run among the hills, the torrents which rush adown the mountains, and the flowing rivers which enrich the plains. One would have said, If he were thirsty he would not tell us, for all the clouds and rains would be glad to refresh his brow, and the brooks and streams would joyously flow at his feet. And yet, though he was Lord of all he had so fully taken upon himself the form of a servant and was so perfectly made in the likeness of sinful flesh, that he cried with fainting voice, " I thirst." How truly man he is ; he is, indeed, " bone of our bone and flesh of our flesh," for he bears our infirmities. I invite you to meditate upon the true humanity of our Lord very reverently, and very lovingly. Jesus was proved to be really man, because he suffered the pains which belong to manhood. Angels cannot suffer thirst. A phantom, as some have called him, could not suffer in this fashion : but Jesus really suffered, not only the more refined pains of delicate and sensitive minds, but the rougher and commoner pangs of flesh and blood. Thirst is a common-place misery, such as may happen to peasants or beggars; it is a real pain, and not a thing of a fancy or a nightmare of dreamland. Thirst is no royal grief, but an evil of universal manhood ; Jesus is brother to the poorest and most humble of our race. Our Lord, however, endured thirst to an extreme degree, for it was the thirst of death which was upon him, and more, it was the thirst of one whose death was not a common one, for "he tasted death for every man." That thirst was caused, perhaps, in part by the loss of blood, and by the fever created by the irritation caused by his four grievous wounds. The nails were fastened in the most sensitive parts of the body, and the wounds were widened as the weight of his body dragged the nails through his blessed flesh, and tore his tender nerves. The extreme tension produced a burning feverishness. It was pain that dried his mouth and made it like an oven, till he declared, in the language of the twenty-second psalm, "My tongue cleaveth to my jaws." It was a thirst such as none of us have ever known, for not yet has the death dew condensed upon our brows. We shall perhaps know it in our measure in our dying hour, but not yet, nor ever so terribly as he did. Our Lord felt that grievous drought of dissolution by which all moisture seems dried up, and the flesh returns to the dust of death: this those know who have commenced to tread the valley of the shadow of death. Jesus, being a man, escaped none of the ills which are allotted to man in death. He is indeed "Immanuel, God with us" everywhere.

Believing this, let us tenderly feel how very near akin to us our Lord Jesus has become. You have been ill, and you have been parched with fever as he was, and then you too have gasped out "I thirst." Your path runs hard by that of your Master. He said, "I thirst," in order that some one might bring him drink, even as you have wished to have a cooling draught handed to you when you could not help yourself. Can you help feeling how very near Jesus is to us when his lips must be moistened with a sponge, and he must be so dependent upon others as to ask drink from their hand? Next time your fevered lips murmur "I am very thirsty," you may say to yourself, "Those are sacred words, for my Lord spake in that fashion." The words, "I thirst," are a common voice in death chambers. We can never forget the painful scenes of which we have been witness, when we have watched the dissolving of the human frame. Some of those whom we loved very dearly we have seen quite unable to help themselves; the death sweat has been upon them, and this has been one of the marks of their approaching dissolution, that they have been parched with thirst, and could only mutter between their half-closed lips, "Give me to drink." Ah, beloved, our Lord was so truly man that all our griefs remind us of him: the next time we are thirsty we may gaze upon him; and whenever we see a friend faint and thirsting while dying we may behold our Lord dimly, but truly, mirrored in his members. How near akin the thirsty Saviour is to us; let us love him more and more.

How great the love which led him to such a condescension as this! Do not let us forget the infinite distance between the Lord of glory on his throne and the Crucified dried up with thirst. A river of the water of life, pure as crystal, proceedeth to-day out of the throne of God and of the Lamb, and yet once he condescended to say, "I thirst." He is Lord of fountains and all deeps, but not a cup of cold water was placed to his lips. Oh, if he had at any time said, "I thirst," before his angelic guards, they would surely have emulated the courage of the men of David when they cut their way to the well of Bethlehem that was within the gate, and drew water in jeopardy of their lives. Who among us would not willingly pour out his soul unto death if he might but give refreshment to the Lord ? And yet he placed himself for our sakes into a position of shame and suffering where none would wait upon him, but when he cried, " I thirst," they gave him vinegar to drink. Glorious stoop of our exalted Head ! O Lord Jesus, we love thee and we worship thee ! We would fain lift thy name on high in grateful remembrance of the depths to which thou didst descend !

While thus we admire his condescension let our thoughts also turn with delight to his sure sympathy : for if Jesus said, " I thirst," then he knows all our frailties and woes. The next time we are in pain or are suffering depression of spirit we will remember that our Lord understands it all, for he has had practical, personal experience of it. Neither in torture of body nor in sadness of heart are we deserted by our Lord ; his line is parallel with ours. The arrow which has lately pierced thee, my brother, was first stained with his blood. The cup of which thou art made to drink, though it be very bitter, bears the mark of his lips about its brim. He hath traversed the mournful way before thee, and every footprint thou leavest in the sodden soil is stamped side by side with his footmarks. Let the sympathy of Christ, then, be fully believed in and deeply appreciated, since he said, " I thirst."

Henceforth, also, let us cultivate the spirit of resignation, for we may well rejoice to carry a cross which his shoulders have borne before us. Beloved, if our Master said, " I thirst," do we expect every day to drink of streams from Lebanon ? He was innocent, and yet he thirsted ; shall we marvel if guilty ones are now and then chastened ? If he was so poor that his garments were stripped from him, and he was hung up upon the tree, penniless and friendless, hungering and thirsting, will you henceforth groan and murmur because you bear the yoke of poverty and want ? There is bread upon your table to-day, and there will be at least a cup of cold water to refresh you. You are not, therefore, so poor as he. Complain not, then. Shall the servant be above his Master, or the disciple above his Lord ? Let patience have her perfect work. You do suffer. Perhaps, dear sister, you carry about with you a gnawing disease which eats at your heart, but Jesus took our sicknesses, and his cup was more bitter than yours. In your chamber let the gasp of your Lord as he said, " I thirst," go through your ears, and as you hear it let it touch your heart and cause you to gird up yourself and say, " Doth he say, ' I thirst ' ? Then I will thirst with him and not complain, I will suffer with him and not murmur." The Redeemer's cry of " I thirst " is a solemn lesson of patience to his afflicted.

Once again, as we think of this " I thirst," which proves our Lord's humanity, let us resolve to shun no denials, but rather court them that we may be conformed to his image. May we not be half ashamed of our pleasures when he says, " I thirst " ? May we not despise our loaded table while he is so neglected ? Shall it ever be a hardship to be denied the satisfying draught when he said, " I thirst." Shall carnal appetites be indulged and bodies pampered when Jesus cried " I thirst " ? What if the bread be dry, what if the medicine be nauseous ; yet for his thirst there was no relief but gall and vinegar, and dare we complain ? For his sake we may rejoice in self-denials, and accept Christ and a crust as all we desire between here and heaven. A Christian living to indulge the base appetites of a brute beast, to eat and to drink almost to gluttony and drunkenness, is utterly unworthy of the name. The conquest of the appetites, the entire subjugation of the flesh, must be achieved, for before our great Exemplar said, "It is finished," wherein methinks he reached the greatest height of all, he stood as only upon the next lower step to that elevation, and said, "I thirst." The power to suffer for another, the capacity to be self-denying even to an extreme to accomplish some great work for God—this is a thing to be sought after, and must be gained before our work is done, and in this Jesus is before us our example and our strength.

Thus have I tried to spy out a measure of teaching, by using that one glass for the soul's eye, through which we look upon "I thirst" as the ensign of his true humanity.

II. Secondly, we shall regard these words, "I thirst," as THE TOKEN OF HIS SUFFERING SUBSTITUTION. The great Surety says, "I thirst," because he is placed in the sinner's stead, and he must therefore undergo the penalty of sin for the ungodly. "My God, my God, why hast thou forsaken me?" points to the anguish of his soul; "I thirst" expresses in part the torture of his body; and they were both needful, because it is written of the God of justice that he is "able to destroy both soul and body in hell," and the pangs that are due to law are of both kinds, touching both heart and flesh. See, brethren, where sin begins, and mark that there it ends. It began with the mouth of appetite, when it was sinfully gratified, and it ends when a kindred appetite is graciously denied. Our first parents plucked forbidden fruit, and by eating slew the race. Appetite was the door of sin, and therefore in that point our Lord was put to pain. With "I thirst" the evil is destroyed and receives its expiation. I saw the other day the emblem of a serpent with its tail in its mouth, and if I carry it a little beyond the artist's intention the symbol may set forth appetite swallowing up itself. A carnal appetite of the body, the satisfaction of the desire for food, first brought us down under the first Adam, and now the pang of thirst, the denial of what the body craved for, restores us to our place.

Nor is this all. We know from experience that the present effect of sin in every man who indulges in it is thirst of soul. The mind of man is like the daughters of the horseleech, which cry for ever "Give, give." Metaphorically understood, thirst is dissatisfaction, the craving of the mind for something which it has not, but which it pines for. Our Lord says, "If any man thirst, let him come unto me and drink," that thirst being the result of sin in every ungodly man at this moment. Now Christ standing in the stead of the ungodly suffers thirst as a type of his enduring the result of sin. More solemn still is the reflection that according to our Lord's own teaching, thirst will also be the eternal result of sin, for he says concerning the rich glutton, "In hell he lift up his eyes, being in torment," and his prayer, which was denied him, was, "Father Abraham, send Lazarus, that he may dip the tip of his finger in water and cool my tongue, for I am tormented in this flame." Now recollect, if Jesus had not thirsted, every one of us would have thirsted for ever afar off from God, with an impassable gulf between us and heaven. Our sinful tongues, blistered by the fever of passion, must have burned for ever had not his tongue been tormented with thirst in our stead. I suppose that the "I thirst" was uttered softly, so that perhaps only one and another who stood near the cross heard it at all; in contrast with the louder cry of "*Lama sabachthani*" and the triumphant shout of "It is finished": but that soft, expiring sigh, "I thirst," has ended for us the thirst which else, insatiably fierce, had preyed upon us throughout eternity. Oh, wondrous substitution of the just for the unjust, of God for man, of the perfect Christ for us guilty, hell-deserving rebels. Let us magnify and bless our Redeemer's name.

It seems to me very wonderful that this "I thirst" should be, as it were, the clearance of it all. He had no sooner said "I thirst," and sipped the vinegar, than he shouted, "It is finished"; and all was over: the battle was fought and the victory won for ever, and our great Deliverer's thirst was the sign of his having smitten the last foe. The flood of his grief had passed the high-water mark, and began to be assuaged. The "I thirst" was the bearing of the last pang; what if I say it was the expression of the fact that his pangs had at last begun to cease, and their fury had spent itself, and left him able to note his lesser pains? The excitement of a great struggle makes men forget thirst and faintness; it is only when all is over that they come back to themselves and note the spending of their strength. The great agony of being forsaken by God was over, and he felt faint when the strain was withdrawn. I like to think of our Lord's saying, "It is finished," directly after he had exclaimed, "I thirst"; for these two voices come so naturally together. Our glorious Samson had been fighting our foes; heaps upon heaps he had slain his thousands, and now like Samson he was sore athirst. He sipped of the vinegar, and he was refreshed, and no sooner has he thrown off the thirst than he shouted like a conqueror, "It is finished," and quitted the field, covered with renown. Let us exult as we see our Substitute going through with his work even to the bitter end, and then with a "Consummatum est" returning to his Father, God. O souls, burdened with sin, rest ye here, and resting live.

III. We will now take the text in a third way, and may the Spirit of God instruct us once again. The utterance of "I thirst" brought out A TYPE OF MAN'S TREATMENT OF HIS LORD. It was a confirmation of the Scripture testimony with regard to man's natural enmity to God. According to modern thought man is a very fine and noble creature, struggling to become better. He is greatly to be commended and admired, for his sin is said to be a seeking after God, and his superstition is a struggling after light. Great and worshipful being that he is, truth is to be altered for him, the gospel is to be modulated to suit the tone of his various generations, and all the arrangements of the universe are to be rendered subservient to his interests. Justice must fly the field lest it be severe to so deserving a being; as for punishment, it must not be whispered to his ears polite. In fact, the tendency is to exalt man above God and give him the highest place. But such is not the truthful estimate of man according to the Scriptures : there man is a fallen creature, with a carnal mind which cannot be reconciled to God ; a worse than brutish creature, rendering evil for good, and treating his God with vile ingratitude. Alas, man is the slave and the dupe of Satan, and a black-hearted traitor to his God. Did not the prophecies say that man would give to his incarnate God gall to eat and vinegar to drink ? It is done. He came to save, and man denied him hospitality : at the first there was no room for him at the inn, and at the last there was not one cool cup of water for him to drink ; but when he thirsted they gave him vinegar to drink.   This is man's treatment of his Saviour.   Universal manhood, left to itself, rejects, crucifies, and mocks the Christ of God. This was the act too of man at his best, when he is moved to pity ; for it seems clear that he who lifted up the wet sponge to the Redeemer's lips, did it in compassion. I think that Roman soldier meant well, at least well for a rough warrior with his little light and knowledge.   He ran and filled a sponge with vinegar : it was the best way he knew of putting a few drops of moisture to the lips of one who was suffering so much ; but though he felt a degree of pity, it was such as one might show to a dog ; he felt no reverence, but mocked as he relieved. We read, " The soldiers also mocked him, offering him vinegar."   When our Lord cried, " Eloi, Eloi," and afterwards said, " I thirst," the persons around the cross said, " Let be, let us see whether Elias will come to save him," mocking him ; and, according to Mark, he who gave the vinegar uttered much the same words. He pitied the sufferer, but he thought so little of him that he joined in the voice of scorn.   Even when man compassionates the sufferings of Christ, and man would have ceased to be human if he did not, still he scorns him ; the very cup which man gives to Jesus is at once scorn and pity, for " the tender mercies of the wicked are cruel."   See how man at his best mingles admiration of the Saviour's person with scorn of his claims; writing books to hold him up as an example and at the same moment reject- ing his deity ; admitting that he was a wonderful man, but denying his most sacred mission ; extolling his ethical teaching and then trampling on his blood : thus giving him drink, but that drink vinegar. O my hearers, beware of praising Jesus and denying his atoning sacrifice. Beware of rendering him homage and dishonouring his name at the same time.

Alas, my brethren, I cannot say much on the score of man's cruelty to our Lord without touching myself and you. Have *we* not often given him vinegar to drink ?   Did we not do so years ago before we knew him ?   We used to melt when we heard about his sufferings, but we did not turn from our sins. We gave him our tears and then grieved him with our sins. We thought sometimes that we loved him as we heard the story of his death, but we did not change our lives for his sake, nor put our trust in him, and so we gave him vinegar to drink. Nor does the grief end here, for have not the best works we have ever done, and the best feelings we have ever felt, and the best prayers we have ever offered, been tart and sour with sin ?   Can they be compared to generous wine ? are they not more like sharp vinegar ?   I wonder he has ever received them, as one marvels why he received this vinegar ; and yet he has received them, and smiled upon us for presenting them. He knew once how to turn water into wine, and in matchless love he has often turned our sour drink-offerings into something sweet to himself, though in themselves, methinks, they have been the juice of sour grapes, sharp enough to set his teeth on edge. We may therefore come before him, with all the rest of our race, when God subdues them to repentance by his love, and look on him whom we have pierced, and mourn for him as one that is in bitterness for his firstborn. We may well remember our faults this day,

> " We, whose proneness to forget
> Thy dear love, on Olivet
> Bathed thy brow with bloody sweat ;

> " We, whose sins, with awful power,
> Like a cloud did o'er thee lower,
> In that God-excluding hour ;

> " We, who still, in thought and deed,
> Often hold the bitter reed
> To thee, in thy time of need."

I have touched that point very lightly because I want a little more time to dwell upon a fourth view of this scene. May the Holy Ghost help us to hear a fourth tuning of the dolorous music, "I thirst."

IV. I think, beloved friends, that the cry of "I thirst" was THE MYSTICAL EXPRESSION OF THE DESIRE OF HIS HEART—"I thirst." I cannot think that natural thirst was all he felt. He thirsted for water doubtless, but his soul was thirsty in a higher sense; indeed, he seems only to have spoken that the Scriptures might be fulfilled as to the offering him vinegar. Always was he in harmony with himself, and his body was always expressive of his soul's cravings as well as of its own longings. " I thirst" meant that his heart was thirsting to save men. This thirst had been on him from the earliest of his earthly days. "Wist ye not," said he, while yet a boy, "that I must be about my Father's business?" Did he not tell his disciples, "I have a baptism to be baptized with, and how am I straitened till it be accomplished?" He thirsted to pluck us from between the jaws of hell, to pay our redemption price, and set us free from the eternal condemnation which hung over us ; and when on the cross the work was almost done his thirst was not assuaged, and could not be till he could say, "It is finished." It is almost done, thou Christ of God; thou hast almost saved thy people ; there remaineth but one thing more, that thou shouldst actually die, and hence thy strong desire to come to the end and complete thy labour. Thou wast still straitened till the last pang was felt and the last word spoken to complete the full redemption, and hence thy cry, "I thirst."

Beloved, there is now upon our Master, and there always has been, a thirst after the love of his people. Do you not remember how that thirst of his was strong in the old days of the prophet ? Call to mind his complaint in the fifth chapter of Isaiah, " Now will I sing to my wellbeloved a song of my beloved touching his vineyard. My wellbeloved hath a vineyard in a very fruitful hill : and he fenced it, and gathered out the stones thereof, and planted it with the choicest vine, and built a tower in the midst of it, and also made a winepress therein." What was he looking for from his vineyard and its winepress? What but for the juice of the vine that he might be refreshed? " And he looked that it should bring forth grapes, and it brought forth wild grapes,"—vinegar, and not wine ; sourness, and not sweetness. So he was thirsting then.

According to the sacred canticle of love, in the fifth chapter of the Song of Songs, we learn that when he drank in those olden times it was in the garden of his church that he was refreshed. What doth he say? "I am come into my garden, my sister, my spouse: I have gathered my myrrh with my spice; I have eaten my honeycomb with my honey; I have drunk my wine with my milk; eat, O friends; drink, yea, drink abundantly, O beloved." In the same song he speaks of his church, and says, "The roof of thy mouth is as the best wine for my beloved, that goeth down sweetly, causing the lips of those that are asleep to speak." And yet again in the eighth chapter the bride saith, "I would cause thee to drink of spiced wine of the juice of my pomegranate." Yes, he loves to be with his people; they are the garden where he walks for refreshment, and their love, their graces, are the milk and wine of which he delights to drink. Christ was always thirsty to save men, and to be loved of men; and we see a type of his life-long desire when, being weary, he sat thus on the well and said to the woman of Samaria, "Give me to drink." There was a deeper meaning in his words than she dreamed of, as a verse further down fully proves, when he said to his disciples, "I have meat to eat that ye know not of." He derived spiritual refreshment from the winning of that woman's heart to himself.

And now, brethren, our blessed Lord has at this time a thirst for communion with each one of you who are his people, not because you can do him good, but because he can do you good. He thirsts to bless you and to receive your grateful love in return; he thirsts to see you looking with believing eye to his fulness, and holding out your emptiness that he may supply it. He saith, "Behold, I stand at the door and knock." What knocks he for? It is that he may eat and drink with you, for he promises that if we open to him he will enter in and sup with us and we with him. He is thirsty still, you see, for our poor love, and surely we cannot deny it to him. Come let us pour out full flagons, until his joy is fulfilled in us. And what makes him love us so? Ah, that I cannot tell, except his own great love. He *must* love; it is his nature. He must love his chosen whom he has once begun to love, for he is the same yesterday, to-day, and for ever. His great love makes him thirst to have us much nearer than we are; he will never be satisfied till all his redeemed are beyond gunshot of the enemy. I will give you one of his thirsty prayers—"Father, I will that they also whom thou hast given me be with me where I am, that they may behold my glory." He wants you brother, he wants you, dear sister, he longs to have you wholly to himself. Come to him in prayer, come to him in fellowship, come to him by perfect consecration, come to him by surrendering your whole being to the sweet mysterious influences of his Spirit. Sit at his feet with Mary, lean on his breast with John; yea, come with the spouse in the song and say, "Let him kiss me with the kisses of his mouth, for his love is better than wine." He calls for that: will you not give it to him? Are you so frozen at heart that not a cup of cold water can be melted for Jesus? Are you lukewarm? O brother, if he says, "I thirst" and you bring him a lukewarm heart, that is worse than vinegar, for he has said, "I will spue thee out of my mouth." He can receive vinegar, but not lukewarm love. Come, bring him your warm heart, and let him drink from that purified chalice as much as he wills. Let all your love be his. I know he loves to receive from you, because he delights even in a cup of cold water that you give to one of his disciples ; how much more will he delight in the giving of your whole self to him ? Therefore while he thirsts give him to drink this day.

V. Lastly, the cry of " I thirst " is to us THE PATTERN OF OUR DEATH WITH HIM. Know ye not, beloved,—for I speak to those who know the Lord,—that ye are crucified together with Christ ? Well, then, what means this cry, " I thirst," but this, that we should thirst too ? We do not thirst after the old manner wherein we were bitterly afflicted, for he hath said, " He that drinketh of this water shall never thirst :" but now we covet a new thirst, a refined and heavenly appetite, a craving for our Lord. O thou blessed Master, if we are indeed nailed up to the tree with thee, give us to thirst after thee with a thirst which only the cup of " the new covenant in thy blood " can ever satisfy. Certain philosophers have said that they love the pursuit of truth even better than the knowledge of truth. I differ from them greatly, but I will say this, that next to the actual enjoyment of my Lord's presence I love to hunger and to thirst after him. Rutherford used words somewhat to this effect, " I thirst for my Lord and this is joy ; a joy which no man taketh from me. Even if I may not come at him, yet shall I be full of consolation, for it is heaven to thirst after him, and surely he will never deny a poor soul liberty to admire him, and adore him, and thirst after him." As for myself, I would grow more and more insatiable after my divine Lord, and when I have much of him I would still cry for more ; and then for more, and still for more. My heart shall not be content till he is all in all to me, and I am altogether lost in him. O to be enlarged in soul so as to take deeper draughts of his sweet love, for our heart cannot have enough. One would wish to be as the spouse, who, when she had already been feasting in the banqueting-house, and had found his fruit sweet to her taste, so that she was overjoyed, yet cried out, " Stay me with flagons, comfort me with apples, for I am sick of love." She craved full flagons of love though she was already overpowered by it. This is a kind of sweet whereof if a man hath much he must have more, and when he hath more he is under a still greater necessity to receive more, and so on, his appetite for ever growing by that which it feeds upon, till he is filled with all the fulness of God. " I thirst,"— ay, this is my soul's word with her Lord. Borrowed from his lips it well suiteth my mouth.

> " I thirst, but not as once I did,
> The vain delights of earth to share ;
> Thy wounds, Emmanuel, all forbid
> That I should seek my pleasures there.

> " Dear fountain of delight unknown !
> No longer sink below the brim ;
> But overflow, and pour me down
> A living and life-giving stream."

Jesus thirsted, then let us thirst in this dry and thirsty land where no water is. Even as the hart panteth after the water brooks, our souls would thirst after thee, O God.

Beloved, let us thirst for the souls of our fellow-men. I have already told you that such was our Lord's mystical desire; let it be ours also. Brother, thirst to have your children saved. Brother, thirst I pray you to have your workpeople saved. Sister, thirst for the salvation of your class, thirst for the redemption of your family, thirst for the conversion of your husband. We ought all to have a longing for conversions. Is it so with each one of you? If not, bestir yourselves at once. Fix your hearts upon some unsaved one, and thirst until he is saved. It is the way whereby many shall be brought to Christ, when this blessed soul-thirst of true Christian charity shall be upon those who are themselves saved. Remember how Paul said, " I say the truth in Christ, I lie not, my conscience also bearing me witness in the Holy Ghost, that I have great heaviness and continual sorrow in my heart. For I could wish that myself were accursed from Christ for my brethren, my kinsmen according to the flesh." He would have sacrificed himself to save his countrymen, so heartily did he desire their eternal welfare. Let this mind be in you also.

As for yourselves, thirst after perfection. Hunger and thirst after righteousness, for you shall be filled. Hate sin, and heartily loathe it; but thirst to be holy as God is holy, thirst to be like Christ, thirst to bring glory to his sacred name by complete conformity to his will.

May the Holy Ghost work in you the complete pattern of Christ crucified, and to him shall be praise for ever and ever. Amen.

6. Christ's Dying Word for His Church

"It is finished."—John xix. 30.

IN the original Greek of John's Gospel, there is only one word for this utterance of our Lord. To translate it into English, we have to use three words; but when it was spoken, it was only one,—an ocean of meaning in a drop of language, a mere drop, for that is all that we can call one word. "It is finished." Yet it would need all the other words that ever were spoken, or ever can be spoken, to explain this one word. It is altogether immeasurable. It is high; I cannot attain to it. It is deep; I cannot fathom it. "Finished." I can half imagine the tone in which our Lord uttered this word, with a holy glorying, a sense of relief, the bursting out of a heart that had long been shut up within walls of anguish. "Finished." It was a Conqueror's cry; it was uttered with a loud voice. There is nothing of anguish about it, there is no wailing in it. It is the cry of One who has completed a tremendous labour, and is about to die; and ere he utters his death-prayer, "Father, into thy hands I commend my spirit," he shouts his life's last hymn in that one word, "Finished."

May God the Holy Spirit help me to handle aright this text that is at once so small and yet so great! There are four ways in which I wish to look at it with you. First, I will speak of this dying saying of our Lord *to his glory;* secondly, I will use the text *to the Church's comfort;* thirdly, I will try to handle the subject *to every believer's joy;* and fourthly, I will seek to show how our Lord's words ought to lead *to our own arousement.*

I. First, then, I will endeavour to speak of this dying saying of Christ TO HIS GLORY. Let us begin with that.

Jesus said, "It is finished." Let us glory in him that it is finished. You and I may well do this when we recollect how very few things we have finished. We begin many things; and, sometimes, we begin well. We commence running like champions who must win the race;

but soon we slacken our pace, and we fall exhausted on the course.
The race commenced is never completed. In fact, I am afraid that
we have never finished anything perfectly. You know what we say
of some pieces of work, " Well, the man has done it; but there is no
' finish ' about it." No, and you must begin with "finish", and go
on with " finish ", if you are at last able to say broadly as the Saviour
said without any qualification, " It is finished."

What was it that was finished ? His life-work and his atoning sacrifice on our behalf. He had interposed between our souls and divine
justice, and he had stood in our stead, to obey and suffer on our behalf.
He began this work early in life, even while he was a child. He
persevered in holy obedience three and thirty years. That obedience
cost him many a pang and groan. Now it is about to cost him his
life ; and as he gives away his life to finish the work of obedience to
the Father, and of redemption for us, he says, " It is finished." It
was a wonderful work even to contemplate ; only infinite love would
have thought of devising such a plan. It was a wonderful work to
carry on for so long ; only boundless patience would have continued
at it ; and now that it requires the offering of himself, and the yielding up of his earthly life, only a Divine Saviour, very God of very
God, would or could have consummated it by the surrender of his
breath. What a work it was ! Yet it was finished ; while you and I
have lots of little things lying about that we have never finished.
We have begun to do something for Jesus that would bring him a
little honour and glory ; but we have never finished it. We did mean
to glorify Christ ; have not some of you intended, oh ! so much ?
Yet it has never come to anything ; but Christ's work, which cost him
heart and soul, body and spirit, cost him everything, even to his death
on the cross, he pushed through all that till it was accomplished, and
he could say, " It is finished."

To whom did our Saviour say, " It is finished" ? He said it to all
whom it might concern ; but it seems to me that he chiefly said it to
his Father, for, immediately after, apparently in a lower tone of voice,
he said, " Father, into thy hands I commend my spirit." Beloved, it
is one thing for me to say to you, "I have finished my work,"—
possibly, if I were dying, you might say that I had finished my work ;
but for the Saviour to say that to God, to hang in the presence of
him whose eyes are as a flame of fire, the great Reader and Searcher
of all hearts, for Jesus to look the dread Father in the face, and say,
as he bowed his head, " Father, it is finished ; I have finished the
work which thou gavest me to do,"—oh, who but he could venture to
make such a declaration as that ? We can find a thousand flaws in
our best works ; and when we lie dying, we shall still have to lament
our shortcomings and excesses ; but there is nothing of imperfection
about him who stood as Substitute for us ; and unto the Father himself he can say, concerning all his work, " It is finished." Wherefore,
glorify him to-night. Oh, glorify him in your hearts to-night that,
even in the presence of the Great Judge of all, your Surety and
your Substitute is able to claim perfection for all his service !

Just think also, for a minute or two, now that you have remembered what Jesus finished, and to whom he said that he had finished

it, *how truly he had finished it.* From the beginning to the end of Christ's life there is nothing omitted, no single act of service ever left undone; neither is there any action of his slurred over, or performed in a careless manner. "It is finished," refers as much to his childhood as to his death. The whole of the service that he was to render to God, when he came here in human form, was finished in every single part and portion of it. I take up a piece of a cabinet-maker's work; and it bears a good appearance. I open the lid, and am satisfied with the workmanship; but there is something about the hinge that is not properly finished. Or, perhaps, if I turn it over, and look at the bottom of the box, I shall see that there is a piece that has been scamped, or that one part has not been well planed or properly polished. But if you examine the Master's work right through, if you begin at Bethlehem and go on to Golgotha, and look minutely at every portion of it, the private as well as the public, the silent as well as the spoken part, you will find that it is finished, completed, perfected. We may say of it that, among all works, there is none like it; a multitude of perfections joined together to make up one absolute perfection. Wherefore, let us glorify the name of our blessed Lord. Crown him; crown him; for he hath done his work well. Come, ye saints, speak much to his honour, and in your hearts keep on singing to the praise of him who did so thoroughly, so perfectly, all the work which his Father gave him to do.

In the first place, then, we use our Lord's words to his glory. Much might be said upon such a theme; but time will not permit it now.

II. Secondly, we will use the text TO THE CHURCH'S COMFORT.

I am persuaded that it was so intended to be used, for none of the words of our Lord on the cross are addressed to his Church but this one. I cannot believe that, when he was dying, he left his people, for whom he died, without a word. "Father, forgive them; for they know not what they do," is for sinners, not for saints. "I thirst," is for himself; and so is that bitter cry, "My God, my God, why hast thou forsaken me?" "Woman, behold thy son!" is for Mary. "To day shalt thou be with me in paradise," is for the penitent thief. "Into thy hands I commend my spirit," is for the Father. Jesus must have had something to say, in the hour of death, for his Church; and, surely, this is his dying word for her. He tells her, shouting it in her ear that has become dull and heavy with despair, "It is finished." "It is finished, O my redeemed one, my bride, my well-beloved, for whom I came to lay down my life; it is finished, the work is done!"

> " Love's redeeming work is done;
> Fought the fight, the battle won."

" Christ loved the church, and gave himself for it." John, in the Revelation, speaks of the Redeemer's work as already accomplished, and therefore he sings, " Unto him that loved us, and washed us from our sins in his own blood, and hath made us kings and priests unto God and his Father; to him be glory and dominion for ever and ever. Amen." This truth is full of comfort to the people of God.

And, first, as it concerns Christ, do you not feel greatly comforted to think that he is to be humiliated no longer? *His suffering and shame are finished.* I often sing, with sacred exultation and pleasure, those lines of Dr. Watts,—

> " No more the bloody spear,
>   The cross and nails no more,
> For hell itself shakes at his name,
>   And all the heavens adore.
>
> " There his full glories shine
>   With uncreated rays,
> And bless his saints' and angels' eyes
>   To everlasting days."

I like also that expression in another of our hymns,—

> " Now both the Surety and sinner are free."

Not only are they free for whom Christ became a Surety, but he himself is for ever free from all the obligations and consequences of his suretyship. Men will never spit in his face again; the Roman soldiers will never scourge him again. Judas, where art thou? Behold the Christ sitting upon his great white throne, the glorious King who was once the Man of sorrows! Now Judas, come, and betray him with a kiss! What, man, dare you not do it? Come Pilate, and wash your hands in pretended innocency, and say now that you are guiltless of his blood! Come, ye Scribes and Pharisees, and accuse him; and oh, ye Jewish mob and Gentile rabble, newly-risen from the grave, shout now, "Away with him! Crucify him!" But see! they flee from him; they cry to the mountains and rocks, "Fall on us, and hide us from the face of h m that sitteth on the throne!" Yet that is the face that was more marred than any man's, the face of him whom they once despised and rejected. Are you not glad to think that they cannot despise him now, that they cannot ill-treat him now?

> " 'Tis past,—that agonizing hour
>   Of torture and of shame;"

and Jesus says of it, "It is finished."

We derive further comfort and joy as we think that, not only are Christ's pangs and sufferings finished, but *his Father's will and word have had a perfect completion.* Certain things were written that were to be done; and these are done. Whatsoever the Father required has been rendered. "It is finished." My Father will never say to me, "I cannot save thee by the death of my Son, for I am dissatisfied with his work." Oh, no, beloved; God is well pleased with Christ, and with us in him! There is nothing which was arranged in the eternal mind to be done, yea, not a jot or tittle, but what Christ has done it all. As his eye, that eye that often wept for us, reads down the ancient writing, Christ is able to say, "I have finished the work which my Father gave me to do. Wherefore, be comforted, O my people, for my Father is well pleased with me, and well pleased with you in me!" I like, when I am in prayer, sometimes to say to the great Father, "Father, look on thy Son. Is he not all loveliness? Are there not in him unutterable beauties? Dost thou not delight in him? If thou hast looked on me, and grown sick of me, as well thou mayest, now refresh thyself by looking on thy Well-beloved, delight thyself in him;—

> " ' Him, and then the sinner see,
> Look through Jesus' wounds on me.' "

The perfect satisfaction of the Father with Christ's work for his people, so that Christ could say, " It is finished," is a ground of solid comfort to his Church evermore.

Dear friends, once more, take comfort from this " It is finished," for *the redemption of Christ's Church is perfected.* There is not another penny to be paid for her full release. There is no mortgage upon Christ's inheritance. Those whom he bought with blood are for ever clear of all charges, paid for to the utmost. There was a handwriting of ordinances against us; but Christ hath taken it away, he hath nailed it to his cross. " It is finished," finished for ever. All those overwhelming debts, which would have sunk us to the lowest hell, have been discharged; and they who believe in Christ may appear with boldness even before the throne of God itself. " It is finished." What comfort there is in this glorious truth!

> " Lamb of God! thy death hath given
> Pardon, peace, and hope of heaven:
> ' It is finished;' let us raise
> Songs of thankfulness and praise! "

And I think that we may say to the Church of God that, when Jesus said, " It is finished," *her ultimate triumph was secured.* " Finished!" By that one word he declared that he had broken the head of the old dragon. By his death, Jesus has routed the hosts of darkness, and crushed the rising hopes of hell. We have a stern battle yet to fight; nobody can tell what may await the Church of God in years to come, it would be idle for us to attempt to prophesy; but it looks as if there were to be sterner times and darker days than we have ever yet known; but what of that? Our Lord has defeated the foe; and we have to fight with one who is already vanquished. The old serpent has been crushed, his head is bruised, and we have now to trample on him. We have this sure word of promise to encourage us, " The God of peace shall bruise Satan under your feet shortly." Surely, " It is finished," sounds like the trumpet of victory; let us have faith to claim that victory through the blood of the Lamb, and let every Christian here, let the whole Church of God, as one mighty army, take comfort from this dying word of the now risen and ever-living Saviour, " It is finished." His Church may rest perfectly satisfied that his work for her is fully accomplished.

III. Now, thirdly, I want to use this expression, " It is finished," TO EVERY BELIEVER'S JOY.

When our Lord said, " It is finished," there was something to make every believer in him glad. What did that utterance mean? You and I have believed in Jesus of Nazareth; we believe him to be the Messiah, sent of God. Now, if you will turn to the Old Testament, you will find that the marks of the Messiah are very many, and very complicated; and if you will then turn to the life and death of Christ, you will see in him *every mark of the Messiah plainly exhibited*. Until he had said, "It is finished," and until he had actually died, there was some doubt that there might be some one prophecy unfulfilled; but now that he hangs upon the cross, every mark, and every sign, and every token of his Messiahship have been fulfilled, and he says, "It is finished." The life and death of Christ and the types of the Old Testament fit each other like hand and glove. It would be quite impossible for any person to write the life of a man, by way of fiction, and then in another book to write out a series of types, personal and sacrificial, and to make the character of the man fit all the types; even if he had permission to make both books, he could not do it. If he were allowed to make both the lock and the key, he could not do it; but here we have the lock made beforehand. In all the Books of the Old Testament, from the prophecy in the Garden of Eden right away down to Malachi, the last of the prophets, there were certain marks and tokens of the Christ. All these were so very singular that it did not appear as if they could all meet in one person; but they did all meet in One, every one of them, whether it concerned some minute point or some prominent characteristic. When the Lord Jesus Christ had ended his life, he could say, "It is finished; my life has tallied with all that was said of it from the first word of prophecy even to the last." Now, that ought greatly to encourage your faith. You are not following cunningly-devised fables; but you are following One who must be the Messiah of God, since he so exactly fits all the prophecies and all the types that were given before concerning him.

"It is finished." Let every believer be comforted in another respect, that *every honour which the law of God could require has been rendered to it*. You and I have broken that law, and all the race of mankind has broken it, too. We have tried to thrust God from his throne; we have dishonoured his law; we have broken his commandments wilfully and wickedly; but there has come One who is himself God, the Law-giver, and he has taken human nature, and in that nature he has kept the law perfectly; and inasmuch as the law had been broken by man, he has in the nature of man borne the sentence due for all man's transgressions. The Godhead, being linked with the manhood, gave supreme virtue to all that the manhood suffered; and Christ, in life and in death, has magnified the law, and made it honourable; and God's law at this day is raised to even greater honour than it had before man broke it. The death of the Son of God, the sacrifice of the Lord Jesus Christ, has vindicated the great moral principle of God's government, and made his throne to stand out gloriously before the eyes of men and angels for ever and ever. If hell were filled with men, it would not be such a vindication of divine justice as when God spared not his own Son, but delivered him up for us all, and made him to die, the Just for the unjust, to bring us to God. Now let every believer rejoice in the great fact that, by the death of Christ, the law of God is abundantly honoured. You can be saved without impugning the holiness of God; you are saved without putting any stain upon the divine statute-book. The law is kept, and mercy triumphs, too.

And, beloved, here is included, of necessity, another comforting truth. Christ might well say, "It is finished," for *every solace conscience can need is now given.* When your conscience is disturbed and troubled, if it knows that God is perfectly honoured, and his law vindicated, then it becomes easy. Men are always starting some new theory of the atonement; and one has said lately that the atonement was simply meant as an easement to the conscience of men. It is not so, my brethren; there would be no easing of the conscience by anything that was meant for that alone. Conscience can only be satisfied if God is satisfied. Until I see how the law is vindicated, my troubled conscience can never find rest. Dear heart, are thine eyes red with weeping? Yet look thou to him who hangs upon the tree. Is thy heart heavy even to despair? Look to him who hangs upon the tree, and believe in him. Take him to be thy soul's atoning Lamb, suffering in thy stead. Accept of him as thy Representative, dying thy death that thou mayest live his life, bearing thy sin that thou mayest be made the righteousness of God in him. This is the best *quietus* in the world for every fear that conscience can raise; let every believer know that it is so.

Once more, there is joy to every believer when he remembers that, as Christ said, "It is finished," *every guarantee was given of the eternal salvation of all the redeemed.* It appears to me that, if Christ finished the work for us, he will finish the work in us. If he has undertaken so supreme a labour as the redemption of our souls by blood, and that is finished, then the great but yet minor labour of renewing our natures, and transforming us even unto perfection, shall be finished, too. If, when we were sinners, Christ loved us so as to die for us, now that he has redeemed us, and has already reconciled us to himself, and made us his friends and his disciples, will he not finish the work that is necessary to make us fit to stand among the golden lamps of heaven, and to sing his praises in the country where nothing that defileth can ever enter?

> "The work which his goodness began,
> The arm of his strength will complete;
> His promise is yea and Amen,
> And never was forfeited yet:
> Things future, nor things that are now,
> Not all things below nor above,
> Can make him his purpose forego,
> Or sever my soul from his love."

I believe it, my brethren. He who has said, "It is finished," will never leave anything undone. It shall never be said of him, "This Man began, but was not able to finish." If he has bought me with his blood, and called me by his grace, and I am resting on his promise and power, I shall be with him where he is, and I shall behold his glory, as surely as he is Christ the Lord, and I am a believer in him. What comfort this truth brings to every child of God!

Are there any of you here who are trying to do something to make a righteousness of your own? How dare you attempt such a work when Jesus says, "It is finished"? Are you trying to put a few of your own merits together, a few odds and ends, fig-leaves and filthy

rags of your own righteousness? Jesus says, "It is finished." **Why**
do you want to add anything of your own to what he has completed?
Do you say that you are not fit to be saved? What! have you to
bring some of your fitness to eke out Christ's work? "Oh!" say you,
"I hope to come to Christ one of these days when I get better."
What! What! What! What! Are you to make yourself better,
and then is Christ to do the rest of the work? You remind me of the
railways to our country towns; you know that, often, the station is
half-a-mile or a mile out of the town, so that you cannot get to the
station without having an omnibus to take you there. But my Lord
Jesus Christ comes right to the town of Mansoul. His railway runs
close to your feet, and there is the carriage-door wide open; step in.
You have not even to go over a bridge, or under a subway; there
stands the carriage just before you. This royal railroad carries souls
all the way from hell's dark door, where they lie in sin, up to heaven's
great gate of pearl, where they dwell in perfect righteousness for
ever. Cast yourself on Christ; take him to be everything you need,
for he says of the whole work of salvation, "It is finished."

I recollect the saying of a Scotchwoman, who had applied to be
admitted to the communion of the kirk. Being thought to be very
ignorant, and little instructed in the things of God, she was put back
by the elders. The minister also had seen her, and thought that, at
least for a while, she should wait. I wish I could speak Scotch, so as
to give you her answer, but I am afraid that I should make a mistake
if I tried it. It is a fine language, doubtless, for those who can
speak it. She said something like this, "Aweel, sir; aweel, sir, but
I ken ae thing. As the lintbell opens to the sun, so my heart opens
to the name of Jesus." You have, perhaps, seen the flax-flower shut
itself up when the sun has gone; and, if so, you know that, whenever
the sun has come back, the flower opens itself at once. "So," said
the poor woman, "I ken one thing, that as the flower opens to the
sun, so my heart opens to the name of Jesus." Do you know that,
friends? Do you ken that one thing? Then I do not care if you do
not ken much else; if that one thing is known by you, and if it be
really so, you may be far from perfect in your own estimation, but
you are a saved soul.

One said to me, when she came to join the church, and I asked
her whether she was perfect, "Perfect? Oh, dear no, sir! I wish
that I could be." "Ah, yes!" I replied, "that would just please you,
would it not?" "Yes; it would indeed," she answered. "Well,
then," I said, "that shows that your heart is perfect, and that you
love perfect things; you are pining after perfection; there is a something in you, an 'I' in you, that sinneth not, but that seeketh after
that which is holy; and yet you do that which you would not, and
you groan because you do, and the apostle is like you when he says,
'It is no more I, the real I, that do it, but sin that dwelleth in me.'"
May the Lord put that "I" into many of you to-night, that "I"
which will hate sin, that "I" which will find its heaven in being
perfectly free from sin, that "I" which will delight itself in the
Almighty, that "I" which will sun itself in the smile of Christ, that
"I" which will strike down every evil within as soon as ever it shows

its head! So will you sing that familiar prayer of Toplady's that we have often sung,—

> " Let the water and the blood,
> From thy riven side which flow'd,
> Be of sin the double cure,
> Cleanse me from its guilt and power " !

IV. I close by saying, in the fourth place, that we shall use this text, " It is finished," TO OUR OWN AROUSEMENT.

Somebody once wickedly said, " Well, if Christ has finished it, there is nothing for me to do now but to fold my hands, and go to sleep." That is the speech of a devil, not of a Christian! There is no grace in the heart when the mouth can talk like that. On the contrary, the true child of God says, " Has Christ finished his work for me? Then tell me what work I can do for him." You remember the two questions of Saul of Tarsus. The first enquiry, after he had been struck down, was, " Who art thou, Lord?" And the next was, " Lord, what wilt thou have me to do?" If Christ has finished the work for you which you could not do, now go and finish the work for him which you are privileged and permitted to do. Seek to—

> " Rescue the perishing,
>   Care for the dying,
> Snatch them in pity from sin and the grave;
>   Weep o'er the erring one,
>   Lift up the fallen,
> Tell them of Jesus, the Mighty to save."

My inference from this saying of Christ, " It is finished," is this,— Has he finished his work for me? Then I must get to work for him, and *I must persevere until I finish my work, too;* not to save myself, for that is all done, but because I am saved. Now I must work for him with all my might; and if there come discouragements, if there come sufferings, if there comes a sense of weakness and exhaustion, yet let me not give way to it; but, inasmuch as he pressed on till he could say, " It is finished," let me press on till I, too, shall be able to say, " I have finished the work which thou gavest me to do." You know how men who go fishing look out for the fish. I have heard of a man going to Keston Ponds on Saturday fishing, and stopping all day Sunday, Monday, Tuesday, Wednesday. There was another man fishing there, and the other man had only been there two days. He said, " I have been here two days, and I have only had one bite." " Why!" replied the other, " I have been here ever since last Saturday, and I have not had a bite yet; but I mean to keep on." " Well," answered the other, " I cannot keep on without catching anything." " Oh!" said number one, " but I have such a longing to catch some fish that I shall stop here till I do." I believe that fellow would catch some fish ultimately, if there were any to be caught; he is the kind of fisherman to do it, and we want to have men who feel that they must win souls for Christ, and that they will persevere till they do. It must be so with us, brethren and sisters; we cannot let men go down to hell if there is any way of saving them.

The next inference is, that *we can finish our work, for Christ finished*

his. You can put a lot of " finish " into your work, and you can hold
on to the end, and complete the work by divine grace; and that grace
is waiting for you, that grace is promised to you. Seek it, find it, get
it. Do not act as some do, ah, even some who are before me now!
They served God once, and then they ran away from him. They have
come back again; God bless them, and help them to be more useful!
But future earnest service will never make up for that sad gap in their
earlier career. It is best to keep on, and on, and on, from the com-
mencement to the close; the Lord help us to persevere to the end, till
we can truly say of our life-work, " It is finished " !

One word of caution I must give you. *Let us not think that our work
is finished till we die.* " Well," says one, " I was just going to say of
my work, ' It is finished.' " Were you? Were you? I remember that,
when John Newton wrote a book about grace in the blade, and grace
in the ear, and grace in the full corn in the ear, a very talkative body
said to him, " I have been reading your valuable book, Mr. Newton;
it is a splendid work; and when I came to that part, ' The full corn
in the ear,' I thought how wonderfully you had described me."
"Oh!" replied Mr. Newton, "but you could not have read the
book rightly, for it is one of the marks of the full corn in the ear
that it hangs its head very low." So it is; and when a man, in a careless, boastful spirit, says of his work, " It is finished," I am inclined
to ask, " Brother, was it ever begun? If your work for Christ is
finished, I should think that you never realized what it ought to be."
As long as there is breath in our bodies, let us serve Christ; as long
as we can think, as long as we can speak, as long as we can work, let
us serve him, let us even serve him with our last gasp; and, if it be
possible, let us try to set some work going that will glorify him when
we are dead and gone. Let us scatter some seed that may spring up
when we are sleeping beneath the hillock in the cemetery. Ah, beloved, we shall never have finished our work for Christ until we bow
our heads, and give up the ghost! The oldest friend here has a little
something to do for the Master. Someone said to me, the other day,
" I cannot think why old Mrs. So-and-so is spared; she is quite a
burden to her friends." "Ah!" I replied, " she has something yet
to do for her Lord, she has another word to speak for him." Sister,
look up your work, and get it done; and you, brother, see what
remains of your life-work yet incomplete. Wind off the ends, get all
the little corners finished. Who knows how long it may be before
you and I may have to give in our account? Some are called away
very suddenly; they are apparently in good health one day, and they are
gone the next. I should not like to leave a half-finished life behind
me. The Lord Jesus Christ said, " It is finished," and your heart
should say, " Lord, and I will finish, too; not to mix my work with
thine, but because thou hast finished thine, I will finish mine."

Now may the Lord give us the joy of his presence at his table!
May the bread and wine speak to you much better than I can! May
every heir of heaven see Christ to-night, and rejoice in his finished
work, for his dear name's sake! Amen.

7. "It Is Finished!"

"When Jesus therefore had received the vinegar, he said, It is finished: and he bowed his head, and gave up the ghost."—John xix. 30.

MY brethren, I would have you attentively observe the singular clearness, power, and quickness of the Saviour's mind in the last agonies of death. When pains and groans attend the last hour, they frequently have the effect of discomposing the mind, so that it is not possible for the dying man to collect his thoughts, or having collected them, to utter them so that they can be understood by others. In no case could we expect a remarkable exercise of memory, or a profound judgment upon deep subjects from an expiring man. But the Redeemer's last acts were full of wisdom and prudence, although his sufferings were beyond all measure excruciating. Remark how clearly he perceived the significance of every type! How plainly he could read with dying eye those divine symbols which the eyes of angels could only desire to look into! He saw the secrets which have bewildered sages and astonished seers, all fulfilled in his own body. Nor must we fail to observe the power and comprehensiveness by which he grasped the chain which binds the shadowy past with the sun-lit present. We must not forget the brilliance of that intelligence which threaded all the ceremonies and sacrifices on one string of thought, beheld all the prophecies as one great revelation, and all the promises as the heralds of one person, and then said of the whole, "'It is finished,' finished in me." What quickness of mind was that which enabled him to traverse all the centuries of prophecy; to penetrate the eternity of the covenant, and then to anticipate the eternal glories! And all this when he is mocked by multitudes of enemies, and when his hands and feet are nailed to the cross! What force of mind must the Saviour have possessed, to soar above those Alps of Agony, which touched the very clouds. In what a singular mental condition must he have been during the period of his crucifixion, to be able to review the whole roll of inspiration! Now, this remark may not seem to be of any great value, but I think its value lies in certain inferences that may be drawn from it. We have sometimes heard it said, "How could Christ, in so short a time, bear suffering which should be equivalent to the torments—the eternal torments of hell?" Our reply is, we are not capable of judging what the Son of God might do even in a moment, much less what he might do and what he might suffer in his life and in his death. It has been frequently affirmed by persons who have been rescued from drowning, that the mind of a drowning man is singularly active. One who, after being some time in the water, was at last painfully restored, said that the whole of his history seemed to come before his mind while he was sinking, and that if any one had asked him how long he had been in the water, he should have said twenty years, whereas he had only been there for a moment or two. The wild romance of Mahomet's journey upon Alborak is not an unfitting illustration. He affirmed that when the angel came in vision to take him on his celebrated journey to Jerusalem, he went through all the seven heavens, and saw all the wonders thereof, and yet he was gone so short a time, that though the angel's wing had touched a basin of water when they started, they returned soon enough to prevent the water from being spilt. The long dream of the epileptic impostor may really have occupied but a second of time. The intellect of mortal man is such that, if God wills it, when it is in certain states, it can think out centuries of thought at once; it can go through in one instant what we should have supposed would have taken years upon years of time for it to know or feel. We think, therefore, that from the Saviour's singular clearness and quickness of intellect upon the cross, it is very possible that he did in the space of two or three hours endure not only the agony which might have been contained in centuries, but even an equivalent for that which might be comprehended in everlasting punishment. At any rate, it is not for us to say that it could not be so. When the Deity is arrayed in manhood, then manhood becomes omnipotent to suffer; and just as the feet of Christ were once almighty to tread the seas, so now was his whole body become almighty to dive into the great waters, to endure an immersion in "unknown agonies." Do not, I pray you, let us attempt to measure Christ's sufferings by the finite line of your own ignorant reason, but let us know and believe that what he endured there was accepted by God as an equivalent for all our pains, and therefore it could not have been a trifle, but must have been all that Hart conceived it to be, when he says He bore—

> "All that incarnate God could bear,
> With strength enough, but none to spare."

My discourse will, I have no doubt, more fully illustrate the remark with which I have commenced; let us proceed to it at once. First, *let us hear the text and understand it;* then *let us hear it and wonder at it;* and then, thirdly, *let us hear it and proclaim it.*

I. LET US HEAR THE TEXT AND UNDERSTAND IT.

The Son of God has been made man. He has lived a life of perfect virtue and of total self-denial. He has been all that life long despised and rejected of men, a man of sorrows and acquainted with grief. His enemies have been legion; his friends have been few, and those few faithless. He is at last delivered over into the hands of them that hate him. He is arrested while in the act of prayer; he is arraigned before both the spiritual and temporal courts. He is robed in mockery, and then unrobed in shame. He is set upon his throne in scorn, and then tied to the pillar in cruelty. He is declared innocent, and yet he is delivered up by the judge who ought to have preserved him from his persecutors. He is dragged through the streets of that Jerusalem which had killed the prophets, and would now crimson itself with the blood of the prophets' Master. He is brought to the cross; he is nailed fast to the cruel wood. The sun burns him. His cruel wounds increase the fever. God forsakes him. "My God, my God, why hast thou forsaken me?" contains the concentrated anguish of the world. While he hangs there in mortal conflict with sin and Satan, his heart is broken, his limbs are dislocated. Heaven fails him, for the sun is veiled in darkness. Earth forsakes him, for "his disciples forsook him and fled." He looks everywhere, and there is none to help; he casts his eye around, and there is no man that can share his toil. He treads the winepress alone; and of the people there is none with him. On, on, he goes, steadily determined to drink the last dreg of that cup which must not pass from him if his Father's will be done. At last he cries—"It is finished," and he gives up the ghost. Hear it, Christians, hear this shout of triumph as it rings to-day with all the freshness and force which it had eighteen hundred years ago! Hear it from the Sacred Word, and from the Saviour's lips, and may the Spirit of God open your ears that you may hear as the learned, and understand what you hear!

1. What meant the Saviour, then, by this—"It is finished?" He meant, first of all, *that all the types, promises, and prophecies were now fully accomplished in him.* Those who are acquainted with the original will find that the words—"It is finished," occur twice within three verses. In the 28th verse, we have the word in the Greek; it is translated in our version "accomplished," but there it stands—"After this, Jesus knowing that all things were now *finished,* that the Scripture might be fulfilled, saith, I thirst." And then he afterwards said, "It is finished." This leads us to see his meaning very clearly, that all the Scripture was now fulfilled, that when he said, "It is finished," the whole book, from the first to the last, in both the law and the prophets, was finished in him. There is not a single jewel of promise, from that first emerald which fell on the threshold of Eden, to that last sapphire-stone of Malachi, which was not set in the breast-plate of the true High Priest. Nay, there is not a type, from the red heifer downward to the turtle-dove, from the hyssop upwards to Solomon's temple itself, which was not fulfilled in him; and not a prophecy, whether spoken on Chebar's bank, or on the shores of Jordan; not a dream of wise men, whether they had received it in Babylon, or in Samaria, or in Judea, which was not now fully wrought out in Christ Jesus. And, brethren, what a wonderful thing it is, that a mass of promises, and prophecies, and types, apparently so heterogeneous, should all be accomplished in one person! Take away Christ for one moment, and I will give the Old Testament to any wise man living, and say to him, "Take this; this is a problem; go home and construct in your imagination an ideal character who shall exactly fit all that

which is herein foreshadowed ; remember, he must be a prophet like unto Moses, and yet a champion like to Joshua ; he must be an Aaron and a Melchisedek ; he must be both David and Solomon, Noah and Jonah, Judah and Joseph. Nay, he must not only be the lamb that was slain, and the scape-goat that was not slain, the turtle-dove that was dipped in blood, and the priest who slew the bird, but he must be the altar, the tabernacle, the mercy-seat, and the shewbread." Nay, to puzzle this wise man further, we remind him of prophecies so apparently contradictory, that one would think they never could meet in one man. Such as these, " All kings shall fall down before him, and all nations shall serve him ;" and yet, " He is despised and rejected of men." He must begin by showing a man born of a virgin mother—" A virgin shall conceive and bear a son." He must be a man without spot or blemish, but yet one upon whom the Lord doth cause to meet the iniquities of us all. He must be a glorious one, a Son of David, but yet a root out of a dry ground. Now, I say it boldly, if all the greatest intellects of all the ages could set themselves to work out this problem, to invent another key to the types and prophecies, they could not do it. I see you, ye wise men, ye are poring over these hieroglyphs ; one suggests one key, and it opens two or three of the figures, but you cannot proceed, for the next one puts you at a nonplus. Another learned man suggests another clue, but that fails most where it is most needed, and another, and another, and thus these wondrous hieroglyphs traced of old by Moses in the wilderness, must be left unexplained, till one comes forward and proclaims, "The cross of Christ and the Son of God incarnate," then the whole is clear, so that he that runs may read, and a child may understand. Blessed Saviour ! In thee we see everything fulfilled, which God spoke of old by the prophets ; in thee we discover everything carried out in substance, which God had set forth us in the dim mist of sacrificial smoke. Glory be unto thy name ! "It is finished"—everything is summed up in thee.

2. But the words have richer meaning. Not only were all types, and prophecies, and promises thus finished in Christ, but *all the typical sacrifices of the old Jewish law, were now abolished as well as explained.* They were finished—finished in him.. Will you imagine for a minute the saints in heaven looking down upon what was done on earth—Abel and his friends who had long ago before the flood been sitting in the glories above. They watch while God lights star after star in heaven. Promise after promise flashes light upon the thick darkness of earth. They see Abraham come, and they look down and wonder while they see God revealing Christ to Abraham in the person of Isaac. They gaze just as the angels do, desiring to look into the mystery. From the times of Noah, Abraham, Isaac, and Jacob, they see altars smoking, recognitions of the fact that man is guilty, and the spirits before the throne say, " Lord, when will sacrifices finish ?—when will blood no more be shed ?" The offering of bloody sacrifices soon increases. It is now carried on by men ordained for the purpose. Aaron and the high priests, and the Levites, every morning and every evening offer a lamb, while great sacrifices are offered on special occasions. Bullocks groan, rams bleed, the necks of doves are wrung, and all the while the saints are crying, " O Lord, how long ?—when shall the sacrifice cease ?" Year after year the high priest goes within the veil and sprinkles the mercy-seat with blood ; the next year sees him do the like, and the next, and again, and again, and again. David offers hecatombs, Solomon slaughters tens of thousands, Hezekiah offers rivers of oil, Josiah gives thousands of the fat of fed beasts, and the spirits of the just say, " Will it never be complete ?—will the sacrifice never be finished ?—must there always be a remembrance of sin ?- will not the last High priest soon come ?—will not the order and line of Aaron soon lay aside its labour, because the whole is finished ?" Not yet, not yet, ye spirits of the just, for after the captivity the slaughter of victims still remains. But lo, he comes ! Gaze more intently than before—He comes who is to close the line of priests ! Lo ! there he stands, clothed—not now with linen ephod, not with ringing bells, nor with sparkling jewels on his breastplate—but arrayed in human flesh he stands, his cross his altar, his body and his soul the victim, himself the priest, and lo ! before his God he offers up his own soul within the veil of thick darkness which hath covered him from the sight of men. Presenting his own blood, he enters within the veil, sprinkles it there, and coming forth from the midst of the darkness, he looks down on the astonished earth, and upward to expectant heaven, and cries, " *It is* finished ! *it is* finished ! "—that for which ye looked so long, is fully achieved and perfected for ever.

3. The Saviour meant, we doubt not, that in this moment *his perfect obedience was finished.* It was necessary, in order that man might be saved, that the law of God should be kept, for no man can see God's face except he be perfect in righteousness

Christ undertook to keep God's law for his people, to obey its every mandate, and preserve its every statute intact. Throughout the first years of his life he privately obeyed, honouring his father and his mother; during the next three years he publicly obeyed God, spending and being spent in his service, till if you would know what a man would be whose life was wholly conformed to the law of God, you may see him in Christ.

> "My dear Redeemer and my Lord,
> I read my duty in thy word,
> But in thy life the law appears
> *Drawn out in living characters.*"

It needed nothing to complete the perfect virtue of life but the entire obedience of death. He who would serve God must be willing not only to give all his soul and his strength while he lives, but he must stand prepared to resign life when it shall be for God's glory. Our perfect substitute put the last stroke upon his work by dying, and therefore he claims to be absolved from further debt, for "it is finished." Yes, glorious Lamb of God, it is finished! Thou hast been tempted in all points like as we are, yet hast thou sinned in none! It *was* finished, for the last arrow out of Satan's quiver had been shot at thee; the last blasphemous insinuation, the last wicked temptation had spent its fury on thee; the Prince of this world had surveyed thee from head to foot, within and without, but he had found nothing in thee. Now thy trial is over, thou hast finished the work which thy Father gave thee to do, and so finished it that hell itself cannot accuse thee of a flaw. And now, looking upon thine entire obedience, thou sayest, "It is finished," and we thy people believe most joyously that it is even so. Brothers and sisters, this is more than you or I could have said if Adam had never fallen. If we had been in the garden of Eden to-day, we could never have boasted a finished righteousness, since a creature can never finish its obedience. As long as a creature lives it is bound to obey, and as long as a free agent exists on earth it would be in danger of violating the vow of its obedience. If Adam had been in Paradise from the first day until now, he might fall to-morrow. Left to himself there would be no reason why that king of nature should not yet be uncrowned. But Christ the Creator, who finished creation, has perfected redemption. God can ask no more. The law has received all it claims; the largest extent of justice cannot demand another hour's obedience. It is done; it is complete; the last throw of the shuttle is over, and the robe is woven from the top throughout. Let us rejoice, then, in this that the Master meant by his dying cry that his perfect righteousness wherewith he covers us was finished.

4. But next, the Saviour meant *that the satisfaction which he rendered to the justice of God was finished.* The debt was now, to the last farthing, all discharged. The atonement and propitiation were made once for all, and for ever, by the one offering made in Jesu's body on the tree. There was the cup; hell was in it; the Saviour drank it—not a sip and then a pause; not a draught and then a ceasing; but he drained it till there is not a dreg left for any of his people. The great ten-thonged whip of the law was worn out upon his back; there is no lash left with which to smite one for whom Jesus died. The great cannonade of God's justice has exhausted all its ammunition; there is nothing left to be hurled against a child of God. Sheathed is thy sword, O Justice! Silenced is thy thunder, O Law! There remaineth nothing now of all the griefs, and pains, and agonies which chosen sinners ought to have suffered for their sins, for Christ has endured all for his own beloved, and "it is finished." Brethren, *it is more than the damned in hell can ever say.* If you and I had been constrained to make satisfaction to God's justice by being sent to hell we never could have said, "It is finished." Christ has paid the debt which all the torments of eternity could not have paid. Lost souls, ye suffer to-day as ye have suffered for ages past, but God's justice is not satisfied; his law is not fully magnified. And when time shall fail, and eternity shall have been flying on, still for ever, for ever, the uttermost farthing never having been paid, the chastisement for sin must fall upon unpardoned sinners. But Christ has done what all the flames of the pit could not do in all eternity; he has magnified the law and made it honourable, and now from the cross he cries—"It is finished."

5. Once again: when he said, "It is finished," *Jesus had totally destroyed the power of Satan, of sin, and of death.* The champion had entered the lists to do battle for our soul's redemption, against all our foes. He met Sin. Horrible, terrible, all-but omnipotent Sin nailed him to the cross; but in that deed, Christ nailed Sin also to the tree. There they both did hang together—Sin, and Sin's destroyer. Sin destroyed Christ, and

by that destruction Christ destroyed Sin. Next came the second enemy, Satan. He assaulted Christ with all his hosts. Calling up his myrmidons from every corner and quarter of the universe, he said, " Awake, arise, or be for ever fallen ! Here is our great enemy who has sworn to bruise my head ; now let us bruise his heel ! " They shot their hellish darts into his heart ; they poured their boiling cauldrons on his brain ; they emptied their venom into his veins ; they spat their insinuations into his face ; they hissed their devilish fears into his ear. He stood alone, the lion of the tribe of Judah, hounded by all the dogs of hell. Our champion quailed not, but used his holy weapons, striking right and left with all the power of God-supported manhood. On came the hosts ; volley after volley was discharged against him. No mimic thunders were these, but such as might shake the very gates of hell. The conqueror steadily advanced, overturning their ranks, dashing in pieces his enemies, breaking the bow and cutting the spear in sunder, and burning the chariots in the fire, while he cried, " In the name of God will I destroy ye ! " At last, foot to foot, he met the champion of hell, and now our David fought with Goliath. Not long was the struggle ; thick was the darkness which gathered round them both ; but he who is the Son of God as well as the Son of Mary, knew how to smite the fiend, and he did smite him with divine fury, till, having despoiled him of his armour, having quenched his fiery darts, and broken his head, he cried, " It is finished," and sent the fiend, bleeding and howling, down to hell. We can imagine him pursued by the eternal Saviour, who exclaims :—

> " Traitor !
> My bolt shalt find and pierce thee through,
> Though under hell's profoundest wave
> Thou div'st, to seek a shelt'ring grave."

His thunderbolt o'ertook the fiend, and grasping him with both his hands, the Saviour drew around him the great chain. The angels brought the royal chariot from on high, to whose wheels the captive fiend was bound. Lash the coursers up the everlasting hills ! Spirits made perfect come forth to meet him. Hymn the conqueror who drags death and hell behind him, and leads captivity captive ! " Lift up your heads, O ye gates, and be ye lifted up, ye everlasting doors, that the King of glory may come in ! " But stay ; ere he enters, let him be rid of this his burden. Lo ! he takes the fiend, and hurls him down through illimitable night, broken, bruised, with his power destroyed, bereft of his crown, to lie for ever howling in the pit of hell. Thus, when the Saviour cried, " It is finished," he had defeated Sin and Satan ; nor less had he vanquished Death. Death had come against him, as Christmas Evans puts it, with his fiery dart, which he struck right through the Saviour, till the point fixed in the cross, and when he tried to pull it out again, he left the sting behind. What could he do more ? He was disarmed. Then Christ set some of his prisoners free ; for many of the saints arose and were seen of many : then he said to him, " Death, I take from thee thy keys ; thou must live for a little while to be the warder of those beds in which my saints shall sleep, but give me thy keys." And lo ! the Saviour stands to-day with the keys of death hanging at his girdle, and he waits until the hour shall come of which no man knoweth ; when the trump of the archangel shall ring like the silver trumpets of Jubilee, and then he shall say, " Let my captives go free." Then shall the tombs be opened in virtue of Christ's death, and the very bodies of the saints shall live again in an eternity of glory.

> " ' It is finish'd !'
> Hear the dying Saviour cry."

II. Secondly, LET US HEAR AND WONDER.

Let us perceive what mighty things were effected and secured by these words, "It is finished." Thus he *ratified the covenant*. That covenant was signed and sealed before, and in all things it was ordered well, but when Christ said, " It is finished," then the covenant was made doubly sure ; when the blood of Christ's heart bespattered the divine roll, then it could never be reversed, nor could one of its ordinances be broken, nor one of its stipulations fail. You know the covenant was on this wise. God covenants on his part that he would give Christ to see of the travail of his soul ; that all who were given to him should have new hearts and right spirits ; that they should be washed from sin, and should enter into life through him. Christ's side of the covenant was this—" Father, I will do thy will ; I will pay the ransom to the last jot and tittle ; I will give thee perfect obedience and complete satisfaction." Now if this second part of the covenant had never been fulfilled, the first part would have been invalid, but when Jesus said, "It is finished," then there was nothing left to be performed on his part, and now the covenant is all on one side. It is God's "I will," and "They shall." "A new heart will I give you, and a right spirit will I put within you." "I will sprinkle clean water upon you and ye shall be clean." "From all your iniquities will I cleanse you." "I will lead you by a way that ye know not." "I will surely bring them in." The covenant that day was ratified. When Christ said, "It is finished," *his Father was honoured, and divine justice was fully displayed.* The Father always did love his people. Do not think that Christ died to make God the Father loving. He always had loved them from before the foundation of the world, but—"It is finished," took away the barriers which were in the Father's way. He would, as a God of love, and now he could as a God of justice, bless poor sinners. From that day the Father is well pleased to receive sinners to his bosom. When Christ said—"It is finished," *he himself was glorified.* Then on his head descended the all-glorious crown. Then did the Father give to him honours, which he had not before. He had honour as God, but as man he was despised and rejected; now as God and man Christ was made to sit down for ever on his Father's throne, crowned with honour and majesty. Then, too, by "It is finished," *the Spirit was procured for us.*

> "'Tis by the merit of his death
>   Who hung upon the tree,
> The Spirit is sent down to breathe
>   On such dry bones as we."

Then the Spirit which Christ had aforetime promised, perceived **a new and living way** by which he could come to dwell in the hearts of men, and men might come up to dwell with him above. That day too, when Christ said—"It is finished," *the words had effect on heaven.* Then the walls of chrysolite stood fast; then the jasper-light of the pearly-gated city shone like the light of seven days. Before, the saints had been saved as it were on credit. They had entered heaven, God having faith in his Son Jesus. Had not Christ finished his work, surely they must have left their shining spheres, and suffered in their own persons for their own sins. I might represent heaven, if my imagination might be allowed a moment, as being ready to totter if Christ had not finished his work; its stones would have been unloosed; massive and stupendous though its bastions are, yet had they fallen as earthly cities reel under the throes of earthquake. But Christ said, "It is finished," and oath, and covenant, and blood set fast the dwelling-place of the redeemed, made their mansions safely and eternally their own, and bade their feet stand immoveably upon the rock. Nay, more, that word "It is finished!" took effect in the gloomy caverns and depths of HELL. Then Satan bit his iron bands in rage, howling, "I am defeated by the very man whom I thought to overcome; my hopes are blasted; never shall an elect one come into my prison-house, never a blood-bought one be found in my abode." Lost souls mourned that day, for they said—"'It is finished!' and if Christ himself, the substitute, could not be permitted to go free till he had finished all his punishment, then we shall never be free." It was their double death-knell, for they said, "Alas for us! Justice, which would not suffer the Saviour to escape, will never suffer us to be at liberty. It is finished with him, and therefore it shall never be finished for us." That day, too, the earth had a gleam of sunlight cast over her which she had never known before. Then her hill-tops began to glisten with the rising of the sun, and though her valleys still are clothed with darkness, and men wander hither and thither, and grope in the noonday as in the night, yet that sun is rising, climbing still its heavenly steeps, never to set, and soon shall its rays penetrate through the thick mists and clouds, and every eye shall see him, and every heart be made glad with his light. The words "It is finished!" consolidated heaven, shook hell, comforted earth, delighted the Father, glorified the Son, brought down the Spirit, and confirmed the everlasting covenant to all the chosen seed.

III. And now I come to my last point, upon which very briefly. "It is finished!" LET US PUBLISH IT.

Children of God, ye who by faith received Christ as your all in all, tell it every day of your lives that "it is finished." Go and tell it to those who are torturing themselves, thinking through obedience and mortification to offer satisfaction. Yonder Hindoo is about to throw himself down upon the spikes. Stay, poor man! wherefore wouldst thou bleed, for "it is finished"? Yonder Fakir is holding his hand erect till the nails grow through the flesh, torturing himself with fastings and with self-denials. Cease,

cease, poor wretch, from all these pains, for "it is finished!" In all parts of the earth there are those who think that the misery of the body and the soul may be an atonement for sin. Rush to them, stay them in their madness and say to them, "Wherefore do ye this? 'It is finished.'" All the pains that God asks, Christ has suffered; all the satisfaction by way of agony in the flesh that the law demandeth, Christ hath already endured. "It is finished!" And when ye have done this, go ye next to the benighted votaries of Rome, when ye see the priests with their backs to the people, offering every day the pretended sacrifice of the mass, and lifting up the host on high—a sacrifice, they say—"an unbloody sacrifice for the quick and the dead,"— cry, "Cease, false priest, cease! for 'it is finished!' Cease, false worshipper, cease to bow, for 'it is finished!'" God neither asks nor accepts any other sacrifice than that which Christ offered once for all upon the cross. Go ye next to the foolish among your own countrymen who call themselves Protestants, but who are Papists after all, who think by their gifts and their gold, by their prayers and their vows, by their church-goings and their chapel-goings, by their baptisms and their confirmations, to make themselves fit for God; and say to them, "Stop, 'it is finished;' God needs not this of you. He has received enough; why will ye pin your rags to the fine linen of Christ's righteousness? Why will you add your counterfeit farthing to the costly ransom which Christ has paid in to the treasure-house of God? Cease from your pains, your doings, your performances, for 'it is finished;' Christ has done it all." This one text is enough to blow the Vatican to the four winds. Lay but this beneath Popery, and like a train of gunpowder beneath a rock, it shall blast it into the air. This is a thunderclap against all human righteousness. Only let this come like a two-edged sword, and your good works and your fine performances are soon cast away. "It is finished." Why improve on what is finished? Why add to that which is complete? The Bible is finished, he that adds to it shall have his name taken out of the Book of Life, and out of the holy city: Christ's atonement is finished, and he that adds to that must expect the selfsame doom. And when ye shall have told it thus to the ears of men of every nation and of every tribe, tell it to all poor despairing souls. Ye find them on their knees, crying, "O God, what can I do to make recompense for my offences?" Tell them, "It is finished;" the recompense is made already. "O God!" they say, "how can I ever get a righteousness in which thou canst accept such a worm as I am?" Tell them, "It is finished;" their righteousness is wrought out already; they have no need to trouble themselves about adding to it, if "it is finished." Go to the poor despairing wretch, who has given himself up, not for death merely, but for damnation—he who says, "I cannot escape from sin, and I cannot be saved from its punishment." Say to him, "Sinner, the way of salvation is finished once for all." And if ye meet some professed Christians in doubts and fears, tell them, "It is finished." Why, we have hundreds and thousands that really are converted, who do not know that "it is finished." They never know that they are safe. They do not know that "it is finished." They think they have faith to-day, but perhaps they may become unbelieving to-morrow. They do not know that "it is finished." They hope God will accept them, if they do some things, forgetting that the way of acceptance is finished. God as much accepts a sinner who only believed in Christ five minutes ago, as he will a saint who has known and loved him eighty years, for he does not accept men because of any anything they do or feel, but simply and only for what Christ did, and that is finished. Oh! poor hearts! some of you do love the Saviour in a measure, but blindly. You are thinking that you must be this, and attain to that, and then you may be assured that you are saved. Oh! you may be assured of it to-day—if you believe in Christ you are saved. "But I feel imperfections." Yes, but what of that? God does not regard your imperfections, but he covers them with Christ's righteousness. He sees them to remove them, but not to lay them to thy charge. "Ay, but I cannot be what I would be." But what if thou canst not? Yet God does not look at thee, as what thou art in thyself, but as what thou art in Christ.

Come with me, poor soul, and thou and I will stand together this morning, while the tempest gathers, for we are not afraid. How sharp that lightning flash! but yet we tremble not. How terrible that peal of thunder! and yet we are not alarmed, and why? Is there anything in us why we should escape? No, but we are standing beneath the cross – that precious cross, which like some noble lightning-conductor in the storm, takes itself all the death from the lightning, and all the fury from the tempest. We are safe. Loud mayest thou roar, O thundering law, and terribly mayest thou flash, O avenging justice! We can look up with calm delight to all the tumult of the elements, for we are safe beneath the cross.

Come with me again. There is a royal banquet spread ; the King himself sits at the table, and angels are the servitors. Let us enter. And we do enter, and we sit down and eat and drink ; but how dare we do this ? our righteousness are as filthy rags— how could we venture to come here ? Oh, because the filthy rags are not ours any longer. We have renounced our own righteousness, and therefore we have renounced the filthy rags, and now to-day we wear the royal garments of the Saviour, and are from head to foot arrayed in white, without spot or wrinkle or any such thing ; standing in the clear sunlight—black, but comely ; loathsome in ourselves, but glorious in him ; condemned in Adam, but accepted in the Beloved. We are neither afraid nor ashamed to be with the angels of God, to talk with the glorified ; nay, nor even alarmed to speak with God himself and call him our friend.

And now last of all, I publish this to sinners. I know not where thou art this morning, but may God find thee out ; thou who hast been a drunkard, swearer, thief ; thou who hast been a blackguard of the blackest kind ; thou who hast dived into the very kennel, and rolled thyself in the mire—if to-day thou feelest that sin is hateful to thee, believe in Him who has said, " It is finished." Let me link thy hand in mine ; let us come together, both of us, and say, " Here are two poor naked souls, good Lord ; we cannot clothe ourselves ;" and he will give us a robe, for "it is finished." " But, Lord, is it long enough for such sinners, and broad enough for such offenders ? " " Yes," saith he, " it is finished." " But we need washing, Lord ! Is there any-thing that can take away black spots so hideous as ours ?" " Yes," saith he, " here is the bath of blood." " But must we not add our tears to it ?" " No," says he, " no, it is finished, there is enough." " And now, Lord, thou hast washed us, and thou hast clothed us, but we would be still completely clean within, so that we may never sin any more ; Lord, is there a way by which this can be done ?" " Yes," saith he, " there is the bath of water which floweth from the wounded side of Christ." " And, Lord, is there enough there to wash away my guiltiness as well as my guilt ?" " Ay," saith he, " it is finished." " Jesus Christ is made unto you sanctification as well as redemption." Child of God, wilt thou have Christ's finished righteousness this morning, and wilt thou rejoice in it more than ever thou hast done before ? And oh ! poor sinner, wilt thou have Christ or no ? " Ah," saith one, " I am willing enough, but I am not worthy." He does not want any worthiness. All he asks is willingness, for you know how he puts it, " Whoever will let him come." If he has given you willingness, you may believe in Christ's finished work this morning. " Ah ! " say you, " but you cannot mean *me.*" But I do, for it says, " Ho, *every one that thirsteth.*" Do you thirst for Christ ? Do you wish to be saved by him ? " *Every one* that thirsteth,"—not only that young woman yonder, not simply that grey-headed old rebel yonder who has long despised the Saviour, but this mass below, and you in these double tiers of gallery—" Every one that thirsteth, come ye to the waters, and he that hath no money come." O that I could " compel" you to come ! Great God, do thou make the sinner willing to be saved, for he wills to be damned, and will not come unless thou change his will ! Eternal Spirit, source of light, and life, and grace, come down and bring the strangers home ! " It is finished.' Sinner, there is nothing for God to do. " It is finished ;" there is nothing for you to do. " It is finished ;" Christ need not bleed. " It is finished ;" you need not weep. " It is finished ;" God the Holy Spirit need not tarry because of your unworthiness, nor need you tarry because of your helplessness. " It is finished ;" every stumbling-block is rolled out of the road ; every gate is opened ; the bars of brass are broken, the gates of iron are burst asunder. " It is finished ;" come and welcome, come and welcome ! The table is laid ; the fatlings are killed ; the oxen are ready. Lo ! here stands the messenger ! Come from the highways and from the hedges ; come from the dens and from the kens of London ; come, ye vilest of the vile ; ye who hate yourselves to-day, come ! Jesus bids you ; oh ! will you tarry ? Oh ! Spirit of God, do thou repeat the invitation, and make it an effectual call to many a heart, for Jesus' sake ! Amen.

8. The Last Words of Christ on the Cross

"And when Jesus had cried with a loud voice, he said, Father, into thy hands I commend my spirit : and having said thus, he gave up the ghost."—Luke xxiii. 46.

"Into thine hand I commit my spirit : thou hast redeemed me, O LORD God of truth."—Psalm xxxi. 5.

"And they stoned Stephen, calling upon God, and saying, Lord Jesus, receive my spirit."—Acts vii. 59.

THIS morning, dear friends, I spoke upon the first recorded words of our Lord Jesus when he said to his mother and to Joseph, "How is it that ye sought me? wist ye not that I must be about my Father's business?" Now, by the help of the blessed Spirit, we will consider the last words of our Lord Jesus before he gave up the ghost, and with them we will examine two other passages in which similar expressions are used.

The words, "Father, into thy hands I commend my spirit," if we judge them to be the last which our Saviour uttered before his death, ought to be coupled with those other words, "It is finished," which some have thought were actually the last he used. I think it was not so; but, anyhow, these utterances must have followed each other very quickly, and we may blend them together, and then we shall see how very similar they are to his first words as we explained them this morning. There is the cry, "It is finished," which you may read in connection with our Authorized Version : "Wist ye not that I must be about my Father's business?" That business was all finished; he had been about it all his life, and now that he had come to the end of his days, there was nothing left undone, and he could say to his Father, "I have finished the work which thou gavest me to do." Then if you take the other utterance of our Lord on the cross, "Father, into thy hands I commend my spirit," see how well it agrees with the other reading of our morning text, "Wist ye not that I must be in my Father's house?" Jesus is putting himself into the Father's hands because he had always desired to be there,—in the Father's house with the Father; and now he is committing his spirit, as a sacred trust, into the Father's hands that he may depart to be with the Father, to abide in his house, and go no more out for ever.

Christ's life is all of a piece, just as the alpha and the omega are letters of the same alphabet. You do not find him one thing at the first, another thing afterwards, and a third thing still later; but he is "Jesus Christ; the same yesterday, and to-day, and for ever." There is a wondrous similarity about everything that Christ said and did. You never need write the name "Jesus" under any one of his sayings, as you have to put the names of human writers under their sayings, for there is no mistaking any sentence that he has uttered.

If there is anything recorded as having been done by Christ, a believing child can judge whether it is authentic or not. Those miserable false gospels that were brought out did very little if any mischief, because nobody, with any true spiritual discernment, was ever duped into believing them to be genuine. It is possible to manufacture a spurious coin which will, for a time, pass for a good one; but it is not possible to make even a passable imitation of what Jesus Christ has said and done. Everything about Christ is like himself; there is a Christlikeness about it which cannot be mistaken. This morning, for instance, when I preached about the Holy Child Jesus, I am sure you must have felt that there was never such another child as he was; and in his death he was as unique as in his birth, and childhood, and life. There was never another who died as he did, and there was never another who lived altogether as he did. Our Lord Jesus Christ stands by himself; some of us try to imitate him, but how feebly do we follow in his steps! The Christ of God still standeth by himself, and there is no possible rival to him.

I have already intimated to you that I am going to have three texts for my sermon; but when I have spoken upon all three of them, you will see that they are so much alike that I might have been content with one of them.

I. I invite you first to consider OUR SAVIOUR'S WORDS JUST BEFORE HIS DEATH: "Father, into thy hands I commend my spirit."

Here observe, first, *how Christ lives and passes away in the atmosphere of the Word of God.* Christ was a grand original thinker, and he might always have given us words of his own. He never lacked suitable language, for "never man spake like this Man." Yet you must have noticed how continually he quoted Scripture; the great majority of his expressions may be traced to the Old Testament. Even where they are not exact quotations, his words drop into Scriptural shape and form. You can see that the Bible has been his one Book. He is evidently familiar with it from the first page to the last, and not with its letter only, but with the innermost soul of its most secret sense; and, therefore, when dying, it seemed but natural for him to use a passage from a Psalm of David as his expiring words. In his death, he was not driven beyond the power of quiet thought, he was not unconscious, he did not die of weakness, he was strong even while he was dying. It is true that he said "I thirst;" but, after he had been a little refreshed, he cried with a loud voice, as only a strong man could, "It is finished." And now, ere he bows his head in the silence of death, he utters his final words, "Father, into thy hands I commend my spirit." Our Lord might, I say again, have made an original speech as his dying declaration; his mind was clear, and calm, and undisturbed; in fact, he was perfectly happy, for he had said, "It is finished." So his sufferings were over, and he was already beginning to enjoy a taste of the sweets of victory; yet, with all that clearness of mind, and freshness of intellect, and fluency of words that might have been possible to him, he did not invent a new sentence, but he went to the Book of Psalms, and took from the Holy Spirit this expression, "Into thy hands I commit my spirit."

How instructive to us is this great truth that the Incarnate Word lived on the Inspired Word! It was food to him, as it is to us; and, brothers and sisters, if Christ thus lived upon the Word of God, should not you and I do the same? He, in some respects, did not need this Book as much as we do. The Spirit of God rested upon him without measure, yet he loved the Scripture, and he went to it, and studied it, and used its expressions continually. Oh, that you and I might get into the very heart of the Word of God, and get that Word into ourselves! As I have seen the silkworm eat into the leaf, and consume it, so ought we to do with the Word of the Lord; — not crawl over its surface, but eat right into it till we have taken it into our inmost parts. It is idle merely to let the eye glance over the words, or to recollect the poetical expressions, or the historic facts; but it is blessed to eat into the very soul of the Bible until, at last, you come to talk in Scriptural language, and your very style is fashioned upon Scripture models, and, what is better still, your spirit is flavoured with the words of the Lord. I would quote John Bunyan as an instance of what I mean. Read anything of his, and you will see that it is almost like reading the Bible itself. He had studied our Authorized Version, which will never be bettered, as I judge, till Christ shall come; he had read it till his very soul was saturated with Scripture; and, though his writings are charmingly full of poetry, yet he cannot give us his *Pilgrim's Progress*—that sweetest of all prose poems—without continually making us feel and say, "Why, this man is a living Bible!" Prick him anywhere; his blood is Bibline, the very essence of the Bible flows from him. He cannot speak without quoting a text, for his very soul is full of the Word of God. I commend his example to you, beloved, and, still more, the example of our Lord Jesus. If the Spirit of God be in you, he will make you love the Word of God; and, if any of you imagine that the Spirit of God will lead you to dispense with the Bible, you are under the influence of another spirit which is not the Spirit of God at all. I trust that the Holy Spirit will endear to you every page of this Divine Record, so that you will feed upon it yourselves, and afterwards speak it out to others. I think it is well worthy of your constant remembrance that, even in death, our blessed Master showed the ruling passion of his spirit, so that his last words were a quotation from Scripture.

Now notice, secondly, that *our Lord, in the moment of his death, recognized a personal God:* "Father, into thy hands I commend my spirit." God is to some men an unknown God. "There may be a God," so they say, but they get no nearer the truth than that. "All things are God," says another. "We cannot be sure that there is a God," say others, "and therefore it is no use our pretending to believe in him, and so to be, possibly, influenced by a supposition." Some people say, "Oh, certainly, there is a God, but he is very far off! He does not come near to us, and we cannot imagine that he will interfere in our affairs." Ah! but our blessed Lord Jesus Christ believed in no such impersonal, pantheistic, dreamy, far-off God; but in One to whom he said, "Father, into thy hands I commend my spirit." His language shows that he realized the personality of God as much as I should recognize the personality of a banker if I said to him, "Sir, I commit that money into your hands." I know that I should not say such a thing as that to a mere dummy, or to an abstract something or nothing; but to a living man I should say it, and I should say it only to a living man. So, beloved, men do not commit their souls into the keeping of impalpable nothings; they do not, in death, smile as they resign themselves to the infinite unknown, the cloudy Father of everything, who may himself be nothing or everything. No, no; we only trust what we know; and so Jesus knew the Father, and knew him to be a real Person having hands, into those hands he commended his departing spirit. I am not now speaking materially, mark you, as though God had hands like ours; but he is an actual Being, who has powers of action, who is able to deal with men as he pleases, and who is willing to take possession of their spirits, and to protect them for ever and ever. Jesus speaks like one who believed that; and I pray that, both in life and in death, you and I may ever deal with God in the same way. We have far too much fiction in religion, and a religion of fiction will bring only fictitious comfort in the dying hour. Come to solid facts, man. Is God as real to thee as thou art to thyself? Come now; dost thou speak with him "as a man speaketh unto his friend"? Canst thou trust him, and rely upon him as thou dost trust and rely upon the partner of thy bosom? If thy God be unreal, thy religion is unreal. If thy God be a dream, thy hope will be a dream; and woe be unto thee when thou shalt wake up out of it! It was not so that Jesus trusted. "Father," said he, "into thy hands I commend my spirit."

But, thirdly, here is a better point still. Observe how *Jesus Christ here brings out the Fatherhood of God.* The Psalm from which he quoted did not say, "Father." David did not get as far as that in words, though in spirit he often did; but Jesus had the right to alter the Psalmist's words. He can improve on Scripture, though you and I cannot. He did not say, "O God, into thine hand I commit my spirit;" but he said, "Father." Oh, that sweet word! That was the gem of our thought, this morning, that Jesus said, "Wist ye not that I must be at my Father's,—that I must be in my Father's house?" Oh, yes! the Holy Child knew that he was specially, and in a peculiar sense, the Son of the Highest; and therefore he said, "My

Father;" and, in dying, his expiring heart was buoyed up and comforted with the thought that God was his Father. It was because he said that God was his Father that they put him to death, yet he still stood to it even in his dying hour, and said, "Father, into thy hands I commend my spirit."

What a blessed thing it is for us also, my brethren, to die conscious that we are sons of God! Oh, how sweet, in life and in death, to feel in our soul the spirit of adoption whereby we cry, "Abba, Father"! In such a case as that,—

"It is not death to die."

Quoting the Saviour's words, "It is finished," and relying upon his Father and our Father, we may go even into the jaws of death without the "quivering lips" of which we sang just now. Joyful, with all the strength we have, our lips may confidently sing, challenging death and the grave to silence our ever-rising and swelling music. O my Father, my Father, if I am in thy hands, I may die without fear!

There is another thought, however, which is perhaps the chief one of all. From this passage, we learn that *our Divine Lord cheerfully rendered up his soul to his Father when the time had come for him to die:* "Father, into thy hands I commend my spirit." None of us can, with strict propriety, use these words. When we come to die, we may perhaps utter them, and God will accept them; these were the very death-words of Polycarp, and Bernard, and Luther, and Melancthon, and Jerome of Prague, and John Huss, and an almost endless list of saints: "Into thy hands I commit my spirit." The Old Testament rendering of the passage, or else our Lord's version of it, has been turned into a Latin prayer, and commonly used among Romanists almost as a charm; they have repeated the Latin words when dying, or, if they were unable to do so, the priest repeated the words for them, attaching a sort of magical power to that particular formula. But, in the sense in which our Saviour uttered these words, we cannot any of us fully use them. We can commit or commend our spirit to God; but yet, brethren, remember that, unless the Lord comes first, we must die; and dying is not an act on our part. We have to be passive in the process, because it is no longer in our power to retain our life. I suppose that, if a man could have such control of his life, it might be questionable when he should surrender it, because suicide is a crime, and no man can be required to kill himself. God does not demand such action as that at any man's hand; and, in a certain sense, that is what would happen whenever a man yielded himself to death. But there was no necessity for our blessed Lord and Master to die except the necessity which he had taken upon himself in becoming the Substitute for his people. There was not any necessity for his death even at the last moment upon the cross, for, as I have reminded you, he cried with a loud voice when natural weakness would have compelled him to whisper or to sigh. But his life was strong within him; if he had willed to do so, he could have unloosed the nails, and come down into the midst of the crowd that stood mocking him. He died of his own free will, "the

Just for the unjust, that he might bring us to God." A man may righteously surrender his life for the good of his country, and for the safety of others. There have frequently been opportunities for men to do this, and there have been brave fellows who have worthily done it; but, then, all those men would have had to die at some time or other. They were only slightly anticipating the payment of the debt of nature; but, in our Lord's case, he was rendering up to the Father the spirit which he might have kept if he had chosen to do so. "No man taketh it from me," said he concerning his life; "I lay it down of myself;" and there is here a cheerful willingness to yield up his spirit into his Father's hands. It is rather remarkable that none of the Evangelists describe our Lord as dying. He did die, but they all speak of him as giving up the ghost,—surrendering to God his spirit. You and I passively die; but he actively yielded up his spirit to his Father. In his case, death was an act; and he performed that act from the glorious motive of redeeming us from death and hell; so, in this sense, Christ stands alone in his death. But, oh, dear brothers and sisters, if we cannot render up our spirit as he did, yet, when our life is taken from us, let us be perfectly ready to give it up. May God bring us into such a state of mind and heart that there shall be no struggling to keep our life, but a sweet willingness to let it be just as God would have it,—a yielding up of everything to his hands, feeling sure that, in the world of spirits, our soul shall be quite safe in the Father's hand, and that, until the resurrection day, the life-germ of the body will be securely in his keeping, and certain that, when the trumpet shall sound, spirit, soul, and body,—that trinity of our manhood,—shall be re-united in the absolute perfection of our being to behold the King in his beauty in the land that is very far off. When God calls us to die, it will be a sweet way of dying if we can, like our Lord, pass away with a text of Scripture upon our lips, with a personal God ready to receive us, with that God recognized distinctly as our Father, and so die joyously, resigning our will entirely to the sweet will of the ever-blessed One, and saying, "It is the Lord," "my Father," "let him do as seemeth him good."

II. My second text is in the 31st Psalm, at the 5th verse; and it is evidently the passage which our Saviour had in his mind just then: "Into thine hand I commit my spirit: thou hast redeemed me, O Lord God of truth." It seems to me that THESE ARE WORDS TO BE USED IN LIFE, for this Psalm is not so much concerning the believer's death as concerning his life.

Is it not very singular, dear friends, that the words which Jesus uttered on the cross you may still continue to use? You may catch up their echo, and not only when you come to die, but to-night, to-morrow morning, and as long as you are here, you may still repeat the text the Master quoted, and say, "Into thine hand I commit my spirit."

That is to say, first, *let us cheerfully entrust our souls to God*, and feel that they are quite safe in his hands. Our spirit is the noblest part of our being; our body is only the husk, our spirit is the living kernel, so let us put it into God's keeping. Some of you have never yet done that, so I invite you to do it now. It is the act of faith which saves the soul, that act which a man performs when he says, "I trust myself to God as he reveals himself in Christ Jesus; I cannot keep myself, but he can keep me; by the precious blood of Christ he can cleanse me; so I just take my spirit, and give it over into the great Father's hand." You never really live till you do that; all that comes before that act of full surrender is death; but when you have once trusted Christ, then you have truly begun to live. And every day, as long as you live, take care that you repeat this process, and cheerfully leave yourselves in God's hands without any reserve; that is to say, give yourself up to God,—your body, to be healthy or to be sick, to be long-lived or to be suddenly cut off; —your soul and spirit, give them also up to God, to be made happy or to be made sad, just as he pleases. Give your whole self up to him, and say to him, "My Father, make me rich or make me poor, give me eye-sight or make me blind, let me have all my senses or take them away, make me famous or leave me to be obscure; I just give myself up to thee; into thine hand I commit my spirit. I will no longer exercise my own choice, but thou shalt choose my inheritance for me. My times are in thy hands."

Now, dear children of God, are you always doing this? Have you ever done it? I am afraid that there are some, even among Christ's professing followers, who kick against God's will; and even when they say to God, "Thy will be done," they spoil it by adding, in their own mind, "and my will, too." They pray, "Lord, make my will thy will," instead of saying, "Make thy will my will." Let us each one pray this prayer every day, "Into thine hand I commit my spirit." I like, at family prayer, to put myself and all that I have into God's hands in the morning, and then, at night, just to look between his hands, and see how safe I have been, and then to say to him, "Lord, shut me up again to-night; take care of me all through the night-watches. 'Into thine hand I commit my spirit.'"

Notice, dear friends, that our second text has these words at the end of it: "*Thou hast redeemed me*, O Lord God of truth." Is not that a good reason for giving yourself up entirely to God? Christ has redeemed you, and therefore you belong to him. If I am a redeemed man, and I ask God to take care of me, I am but asking the King to take care of one of his own jewels,—a jewel that cost him the blood of his heart.

And I may still more specially expect that he will do so, because of the title which is here given to him: "Thou hast redeemed me, *O Lord God of truth*." Would he be the God of truth if he began with redemption, and ended with destruction;—if he began by giving his Son to die for us, and then kept back other mercies which we daily need to bring us to heaven? No; the gift of his Son is the pledge that he will save his people from their sins, and bring them home to glory; and he will do it. So, every day, go to him with this declaration, "Into thine hand I commit my spirit." Nay, not only every day, but all through the day. Does a horse run away with you? Then you cannot do better than say, "Father, into thine hand I commit my spirit." And if the horse does not run away with you, you cannot do better than say the same words. Have you to go into a house where there is fever; I mean, is it your duty to go there? Then go saying, "Father, into thine hand I commit my spirit." I would advise you to do this every time you walk down the street, or even while you sit in your own house. Dr. Gill, my famous predecessor, spent very much time in his study; and, one day, somebody said to him, "Well, at any rate, the studious man is safe from most of the accidents of life." It so happened that, one morning, when the good man left his familiar arm-chair for a little while, there came a gale of wind that blew down a stack of chimneys, which crashed through the roof, and fell right into the place where he would have been sitting if the providence of God had not just then drawn him away; and he said, "I see that we need divine providence to care for us in our studies just as much as in the streets." "Father, into thy hands I commit my spirit." I have often noticed that, if any of our friends get into accidents and troubles, it is usually when they are away for a holiday; it is a curious thing, but I have often remarked it. They go out for their health, and come home ill; they leave us with all their limbs whole, and return to us crippled; therefore, we must pray God to take special care of friends in the country or by the sea, and we must commit ourselves to his hands wherever we may be. If we had to go into a lazar-house, we should certainly ask God to protect us from the deadly leprosy; but we ought equally to seek the Lord's protection while dwelling in the healthiest place or in our own homes.

David said to the Lord, "Into thine hand I commit my spirit;" but let me beg you to add that word which our Lord inserted, "Father." David is often a good guide for us, but David's Lord is far better; and if we follow him, we shall improve upon David. So, let us each say, "Father, Father, into thine hand I commit my spirit." That is a sweet way of living every day, committing everything to our Heavenly Father's hand, for that hand can do his child no unkindness. "Father, I might not be able to trust thine angels, but I can trust thee." The psalmist does not say, "Into the hand of providence I commit my spirit." Do you notice how men try to get rid of God by saying, "Providence did this," and "Providence did that," and "Providence did the other"? If you ask them, "What is providence?"—they will probably reply, "Well, providence is——providence." That is all they can say. There is many a man who talks very confidently about reverencing nature, obeying the laws of nature, noting the powers of nature, and so on. Step up to that eloquent lecturer, and say to him, "Will you kindly explain to me what nature is?" He answers, "Why, nature, —well, it is—nature." Just so, sir; but, then, what is nature? And he says, "Well,—well,—it is nature;" and that is all you will get out of him. Now, I believe in nature, and I believe in providence; but, at the back of everything, I believe in God, and in the God who has hands;—not in an idol that has no hands, and can do nothing,—but in the God to whom I can say, "'Father, into thine hand I commit my spirit.' I rejoice that I am able to put myself there, for I feel absolutely safe in trusting myself to thy keeping."

So live, beloved, and you shall live safely, and happily; and you shall have hope in your life, and hope in your death.

III. My third text will not detain us many minutes; it is intended to explain to us THE USE OF OUR SAVIOUR'S DYING WORDS FOR OURSELVES. Turn to the account of the death of Stephen, in the 7th chapter of Acts, at the 59th verse, and you will see there how far a man of God may dare to go in his last moments in quoting from David and from the Lord Jesus Christ: "And they stoned Stephen, calling upon God, and saying, Lord Jesus, receive my spirit." So here is a text for us to use when we come to die: "Lord Jesus, receive my spirit." I have explained to you that, strictly, we can hardly talk of yielding up our spirit, but we may speak of Christ receiving it, and say, with Stephen, "Lord Jesus, receive my spirit."

What does this prayer mean? I must just hurriedly give you two or three thoughts concerning it, and so close my discourse. I think this prayer means that, *if we can die as Stephen did, we shall die with a certainty of immortality.* Stephen prayed, "Lord Jesus, receive my spirit." He did not say, "I am afraid my poor spirit is going to die." No; the spirit is something which still exists after death, something which Christ can receive, and therefore Stephen asks him to receive it. You and I are not going upstairs to die as if we were only like cats and dogs; we go up there to die like immortal beings who fall asleep on earth, and open our eyes in heaven. Then, at the sound of the archangel's trumpet, our very body is to rise to dwell again with our spirit; we have not any question about this matter. I think I have told you what an infidel once said to a Christian man, "Some of you Christians have great fear in dying because you believe that there is another state to follow this one. I have not the slightest fear, for I believe that I shall be annihilated, and therefore all fear of death is gone from me." "Yes," said the Christian man, "and in that respect you seem to me to be on equal terms with that bullock grazing over there, which, like yourself, is free from any fear of death. Pray, sir, let me ask you a simple question. Have you any hope?" "Hope, sir? Hope, sir? No, I have no hope; of course, I have no hope, sir." "Ah, then!" replied the other, "despite the fears that sometimes come over feeble believers, they have a hope which they would not and could not give up." And that hope is, that our spirit—even that spirit which we commit into Jesus Christ's hands,—shall be "for ever with the Lord."

The next thought is that, *to a man who can die as Stephen did, there is a certainty that Christ is near,*—so near that the man speaks to him, and says, "Lord Jesus, receive my spirit." In Stephen's case, the Lord Jesus was so near that the martyr could see him, for he said, "Behold, I see the heavens opened, and the Son of man standing on the right hand of God." Many dying saints have borne a similar testimony; it is no strange thing for us to hear them say, before they died, that they could see within the pearly gates; and they have told us this with such evident truthfulness, and with such rapture, or sometimes so calmly, in such a businesslike tone of voice, that we were sure that they were neither deceived nor speaking falsehood. They spake what they knew to be true, for Jesus was there with them. Yes, beloved, before you can call your children about your death-bed, Jesus will be there already, and into his hands you may commit your spirit.

Moreover, *there is a certainty that we are quite safe in his hands.* Wherever else we are insecure, if we ask him to receive our spirit, and he receives it, who can hurt us? Who can pluck us out of his hands? Rouse ye, death and hell! Come forth, all ye powers of darkness! What can you do when once a spirit is in the hands of the omnipotent Redeemer? We must be safe there.

Then there is the other certainty, *that he is quite willing to take us into his hands.* Let us put ourselves into his hands now; and then we need not be ashamed to repeat the operation every day, and we may be sure that we shall not be rejected at the last. I have often told you of the good old woman, who was dying, and to whom someone said, "Are you not afraid to die?" "Oh, no;" she replied, "there is nothing at all to fear. I have dipped my foot in the river of death every morning before I have had my breakfast, and I am not afraid to die now." You remember that dear saint, who died in the night, and who had left written on a piece of paper by her bedside these lines which, ere she fell asleep, she felt strong enough to pencil down,—

> "Since Jesus is mine, I'll not fear undressing,
> But gladly put off these garments of clay;
> To die in the Lord, is a covenant blessing,
> Since Jesus to glory thro' death led the way."

It was well that she could say it, and may we be able to say the same whenever the Master calls us to go up higher! I want, dear friends, that we should all of us have as much willingness to depart as if it were a matter of will with us. Blessed be God, it is not left to our choice, it is not left to our will, when we shall die. God has appointed that day, and ten thousand devils cannot consign us to the grave before our time. We shall not die till God decrees it.

> "Plagues and deaths around me fly,
> Till he please I cannot die;
> Not a single shaft can hit
> Till the God of love sees fit."

But let us be just as willing to depart as if it were really a matter of choice; for, wisely, carefully, coolly, consider that, if it were left to us, we should none of us be wise if we did not choose to go. Apart from the coming of our Lord, the most miserable thing that I know of would be a suspicion that we might not die. Do you know what quaint old Rowland Hill used to say when he found himself getting very old? He said, "Surely they must be forgetting me up there;" and every now and then, when some dear old saint was dying, he would say, "When you get to heaven, give my love to John Berridge, and John Bunyan, and ever so many more of the good Johns, and tell them I hope they will see poor old Rowly up there before long." Well, there was common sense in that wishing to get home, longing to be with God. To be with Christ, is far better than to be here.

Sobriety itself would make us choose to die; well, then, do not let us run back, and become utterly unwilling, and struggle and strive and fret and fume over it. When I hear of believers who do not like to talk about death, I am afraid concerning them. It is greatly wise to be familiar with our resting-place. When I went, recently, to the cemetery at Norwood, to lay the body of our dear brother Perkins there for a little while, I felt that it was a healthy thing for me to stand at the grave's brink, and to walk amid that forest of memorials of the dead, for this is where I, too, must go. Ye living men, come and view the ground where you must shortly lie; and, as it must be so, let us who are believers welcome it.

But what if you are not believers? Ah! that is another matter altogether. If you have not believed in Christ, you may well be afraid even to rest on the seat where you are sitting. I wonder that the earth itself does not say, "O God, I will not hold this wretched sinner up any longer! Let me open my mouth, and swallow him!" All nature must hate the man who hates God. Surely, all things must loathe to minister to the life of a man who does not live unto God. Oh that you would seek the Lord, and trust Christ, and find eternal life! If you have done so, do not be afraid to go forth to live, or to die, just as God pleases.

9. Our Lord's Last Cry from the Cross

"And when Jesus had cried with a loud voice, he said, Father, into thy hands I commend my spirit : and having said thus, he gave up the ghost."—Luke xxiii. 46.

THESE were the dying words of our Lord Jesus Christ, "Father, into thy hands I commend my spirit." It may be instructive if I remind you that the words of Christ upon the cross were seven. Calling each of his cries, or utterances, by the title of a word, we speak of the seven last words of the Lord Jesus Christ. Let me rehearse them in your hearing. The first, when they nailed him to the cross, was, "Father, forgive them ; for they know not what they do." Luke has preserved that word. Later, when one of the two thieves said to Jesus, "Lord, remember me when thou comest into thy kingdom," Jesus said to him, "Verily I say unto thee, To day shalt thou be with me in paradise." This also Luke has carefully preserved. Farther on, our Lord, in his great agony, saw his mother, with breaking heart, standing by the cross, and looking up to him with unutterable love and grief, and he said to her, "Woman, behold thy son !" and to the beloved disciple, "Behold thy mother !" and thus he provided a home for her when he himself should be gone away. This utterance has only been preserved by John.

The fourth and central word of the seven was, "Eloi, Eloi, lama sabachthani ? " which is, being interpreted, "My God, my God, why hast thou forsaken me ? " This was the culmination of his grief, the central point of all his agony. That most awful word that ever fell from the lips of man, expressing the quintessence of exceeding agony, is well put fourth, as though it had need of three words before it, and three words after it, as its body-guard. It tells of a good man, a son of God, *the* Son of God, forsaken of his God. That central word of the seven is found in Matthew and in Mark, but not in Luke or John ; but the fifth word has been preserved by John ; that is, " I thirst," the shortest, but not quite the sharpest of all the Master's words, though under a bodily aspect, perhaps the sharpest of them all. John has also treasured up another very precious saying of Jesus Christ on the cross, that is the wondrous word, " It is finished." This was the last word but one, " It is finished," the gathering up of all his lifework, for he had left nothing undone, no thread was left a-ravelling, the whole fabric of redemption had been woven, like his garment, from the top throughout, and it was finished to perfection. After he had said, " It is finished," he uttered the last word of all, " Father, into thy hands I commend my spirit," which I have taken for a text to-night; but to which I will not come immediately.

There has been a great deal said about these seven cries from the cross by divers writers; and though I have read what many of them have written, I cannot add anything to what they have said, since they have delighted to dwell upon these seven last cries; and here the most ancient writers, of what would be called the Romish school, are not to be excelled, even by Protestants, in their intense devotion to every letter of our Saviour's dying words; and they sometimes strike out new meanings, richer and more rare than any that have occurred to the far cooler minds of modern critics, who are as a rule greatly blessed with moles' eyes, able to see where there is nothing to be seen, but never able to see when there is anything worth seeing. Modern criticism, like modern theology, if it were put in the Garden of Eden, would not see a flower. It is like the sirocco that blasts and burns, it is without either dew or unction; in fact, it is the very opposite of these precious things, and proves itself to be unblest of God, and unblessing to men.

Now concerning these seven cries from the cross, many authors have drawn from them lessons concerning *seven duties*. Listen. When our Lord said, " Father, forgive them," in effect, he said to us, " Forgive your enemies." Even when they despitefully use you, and put you to terrible pain, be ready to pardon them. Be like the sandalwood tree, which perfumes the axe that fells it. Be all gentleness, and kindness, and love; and be this your prayer, " Father, forgive them."

The next duty is taken from the second cry, namely, that of penitence and faith in Christ, for he said to the dying thief, " To day shalt thou be with me in paradise." Have you, like him, confessed your sin? Have you his faith, and his prayerfulness? Then you shall be accepted even as he was. Learn, then, from the second cry, the duty of penitence and faith.

When our Lord, in the third cry, said to his mother, " Woman, behold thy son!" he taught us the duty of filial love. No Christian must ever be short of love to his mother, his father, or to any of those who are endeared to him by relationships which God has appointed for us to observe. Oh, by the dying love of Christ to his mother, let no man here unman himself by forgetting his mother! She bore you; bear her in her old age, and lovingly cherish her even to the last.

Jesus Christ's fourth cry teaches us the duty of clinging to God, and trusting in God: "My God, my God." See how, with both hands, he takes hold of him: " My God, my God, why hast thou forsaken me?" He cannot bear to be left of God; all else causes him but little pain compared with the anguish of being forsaken of his God. So learn to cling to God, to grip him with a double-handed faith; and if thou dost even think that he has forsaken thee, cry after him, and say, "Show me wherefore thou contendest with me, for I cannot bear to be without thee."

The fifth cry, "I thirst," teaches us to set a high value upon the fulfilment of God's Word. "After this, Jesus knowing that all things were now accomplished, that the scripture might be fulfilled, saith, I thirst." Take thou good heed, in all thy grief and weakness, still to preserve the Word of thy God, and to obey the precept, learn the doctrine, and delight in the promise. As thy Lord, in his great anguish said, "I thirst," because it was written that so he would speak, do thou have regard unto the Word of the Lord even in little things.

That sixth cry, "It is finished," teaches us perfect obedience. Go through with thy keeping of God's commandment; leave out no command, keep on obeying till thou canst say, "It is finished." Work thy likework, obey thy Master, suffer or serve according to his will, but rest not till thou canst say with thy Lord, "It is finished." "I have finished the work which thou gavest me to do."

And that last word, "Father, into thy hands I commend my spirit," teaches us resignation. Yield all things, yield up even thy spirit to God at his bidding. Stand still, and make a full surrender to the Lord, and let this be thy watchword from the first even to the last, "Into thy hands, my Father, I commend my spirit."

I think that this study of Christ's last words should interest you; therefore let me linger a little longer upon it. Those seven cries from the cross also teach us something about *the attributes and offices of our Master*. They are seven windows of agate, and gates of carbuncle, through which you may see him, and approach him.

First, would you see him as Intercessor? Then he cries, "Father, forgive them; for they know not what they do." Would you look at him as King? Then hear his second word, "Verily I say unto thee, To day shalt thou be with me in paradise." Would you mark him as a tender Guardian? Hear him say to Mary, "Woman, behold thy son!" and to John, "Behold thy mother!" Would you peer into the dark abyss of the agonies of his soul? Hear him cry, "My God, my God, why hast thou forsaken me?" Would you understand the reality and the intensity of his bodily sufferings? Then hear him say, "I thirst," for there is something exquisite in the torture of thirst when brought on by the fever of bleeding wounds. Men on the battle-field, who have lost much blood, are devoured with thirst, and tell you that it is the worst pang of all. "I thirst," says Jesus. See the Sufferer in the body, and understand how he can sympathize with you who suffer, since he suffered so much on the cross. Would you see him as the Finisher of your salvation? Then hear his cry, "*Consummatum est*"—"It is finished." Oh, glorious note! Here you see the blessed Finisher of your faith. And would you then take one more gaze, and understand how voluntary was his suffering? Then hear him say, not as one who is robbed of life, but as one who takes his soul, and hands it over to the keeping of another, "Father, into thy hands I commend my spirit."

Is there not much to be learnt from these cries from the cross? Surely these seven notes make a wondrous scale of music if we do but know how to listen to them. Let me run up the scale again. Here, first, you have Christ's fellowship with men : " Father, forgive them." He stands side by side with sinners, and tries to make an apology for them : "They know not what they do." Here is, next, his kingly power. He sets open heaven's gate to the dying thief, and bids him enter. "To day shalt thou be with me in paradise." Thirdly, behold his human relationship. How near of kin he is to us! "Woman, behold thy son!" Remember how he says, "Whosoever shall do the will of my Father who is in heaven, the same is my brother, and sister, and mother." He is bone of our bone, and flesh of our flesh. He belongs to the human family. He is more of a man than any man. As surely as he is very God of very God, he is also very man of very man, taking into himself the nature, not of the Jew only, but of the Gentile, too. Belonging to his own nationality, but rising above all, he is the Man of men, the Son of man.

See, next, his taking our sin. You say, "Which note is that?" Well, they are all to that effect; but this one chiefly, "My God, my God, why hast thou forsaken me?" It was because he bore our sins in his own body on the tree that he was forsaken of God. "He hath made him to be sin for us who knew no sin," and hence the bitter cry, "Eloi, Eloi, lama sabachthani?" Behold him, in that fifth cry, "I thirst," taking, not only our sin, but also our infirmity, and all the suffering of our bodily nature. Then, if you would see his fulness as well as his weakness, if you would see his all-sufficiency as well as his sorrow, hear him cry, "It is finished." What a wonderful fulness there is in that note! Redemption is all accomplished; it is all complete; it is all perfect. There is nothing left, not a drop of bitterness in the cup of gall; Jesus has drained it dry. There is not a farthing to be added to the ransom price; Jesus has paid it all. Behold his fulness in the cry, "It is finished." And then, if you would see how he has reconciled us to himself, behold him, the Man who was made a curse for us, returning with a blessing to his Father, and taking us with him, as he draws us all up by that last dear word, " Father, into thy hands I commend my spirit."

"Now both the Surety and sinner are free."

Christ goes back to the Father, for "It is finished," and you and I come to the Father through his perfect work.

I have only practised two or three tunes that can be played upon this harp, but it is a wonderful instrument. If it be not a harp of ten strings, it is, at any rate, an instrument of seven strings, and neither time nor eternity shall ever be able to fetch all the music out of them. Those seven dying words of the ever-living Christ will make melody for us in glory through all the ages of eternity.

I shall now ask your attention for a little time to the text itself: " Father, into thy hands I commend my spirit."

Do you see our Lord? He is dying; and as yet, his face is toward man. His last word to man is the cry, "It is finished." Hear, all ye sons of men, he speaks to you, "It is finished." Could you have a choicer word with which he should say "Adieu" to you in the hour of death? He tells you not to fear that his work is imperfect, not to tremble lest it should prove insufficient. He speaks to you, and declares with his dying utterance, "It is finished." Now he has done with you, and he turns his face the other way. His day's work is done, his more than Herculean toil is accomplished, and the great Champion is going back to his Father's throne, and he speaks; but not to you. His last word is addressed to his Father, "Father, into thy hands I commend my spirit." These are his first words in going home to his Father, as "It is finished," is his last word as, for a while, he quits our company. Think of these words, and may they be your first words, too, when you return to your Father! May you speak thus to your Divine Father in the hour of death! The words were much hackneyed in Romish times; but they are not spoilt even for that. They used to be said in the Latin by dying men, " *In manus tuas, Domine, commendo spiritum meum.*" Every dying man used to try to say those words in Latin; and if he did not, somebody tried to say them for him. They were made into a kind of spell of witchcraft; and so they lost that sweetness to our ears in the Latin; but in the English they shall always stand as the very essence of music for a dying saint, "Father, into thy hands I commend my spirit."

It is very noteworthy that the last words that our Lord used were quoted from the Scriptures. This sentence is taken, as I daresay most of you know, from the thirty-first Psalm, and the fifth verse. Let me read it to you. What a proof it is of how full Christ was of the Bible! He was not one of those who think little of the Word of God. He was saturated with it. He was as full of Scripture as the fleece of Gideon was full of dew. He could not speak even in his death without uttering Scripture. This is how David put it, "Into thine hand I commit my spirit: thou hast redeemed me, O Lord God of truth." Now, beloved, the Saviour altered this passage, or else it would not quite have suited him. Do you see, first, he was obliged, in order to fit it to his own case, to add something to it? What did he add to it? Why, that word, "Father." David said, "Into thine hand I commit my spirit;" but Jesus says, "Father, into thy hands I commend my spirit." Blessed advance! He knew more than David did, for he was more the Son of God than David could be. He was *the* Son of God in a very high and special sense by eternal filiation; and so he begins the prayer with, "Father." But then he takes something from it. It was needful that he should do so, for David said, "Into thine hand I commit my spirit: thou hast redeemed me." Our blessed Master was not redeemed, for he was the Redeemer; and he could have said, "Into thine hand I commit my spirit, for I have redeemed my people;" but that he did not choose to say. He simply took that part which suited himself, and used it as his own, "Father, into thy hands I commend my spirit." Oh, my brethren, you will not do better, after all, than to quote Scripture, especially in prayer. There are no prayers so good as those that are full of the Word of God. May all our speech be flavoured with texts! I wish that it were more so. They laughed at our Puritan forefathers because the very names of their children were fetched out of passages of Scripture; but I, for my part, had much rather be laughed at for talking much of Scripture than for talking much of trashy novels— novels with which (I am ashamed to say it) many a sermon nowadays is larded, ay, larded with novels that are not fit for decent men to read, and which are coated over till one hardly knows whether he is hearing about a historical event, or only a piece of fiction—from which abomination, good Lord, deliver us!

So, then, you see how well the Saviour used Scripture, and how, from his first battle with the devil in the wilderness till his last struggle with death on the cross, his weapon was ever, "It is written."

Now, I am coming to the text itself, and I am going to preach from it for only a very short time. In doing so, firstly, *let us learn the doctrine* of this last cry from the cross; secondly, *let us practise the duty*; and thirdly, *let us enjoy the privilege.*

I. First, LET US LEARN THE DOCTRINE of our Lord's last cry from the cross.

What is the doctrine of this last word of our Lord Jesus Christ? *God is his Father, and God is our Father.* He who himself said, "Father," did not say for himself, "Our Father," for the Father is Christ's Father in a higher sense than he is ours; but yet he is not more truly the Father of Christ than he is our Father if we have believed in Jesus. "Ye are all the children of God by faith in Christ Jesus." Jesus said to Mary Magdalene, "I ascend unto my Father, and your Father; and to my God, and your God." Believe the doctrine of the Fatherhood of God to his people. As I have warned you before, abhor the doctrine of the universal fatherhood of God, for it is a lie, and a deep deception. It stabs at the heart, first, of the doctrine of the adoption, which is taught in Scripture, for how can God adopt men if they are all his children already? In the second place, it stabs at the heart of the doctrine of regeneration, which is certainly taught in the Word of God. Now it is by regeneration and faith that we become the children of God, but how can that be if we are the children of God already? "As many as received him, to them gave he power to become the sons of God, even to them that believe on his name: which were born, not of blood, nor of the will of the flesh, nor of the will of man, but of God." How can God give to men the power to become his sons if they have it already? Believe not that lie of the devil, but believe this truth of God, that Christ and all who are by living faith in Christ may rejoice in the Fatherhood of God.

Next learn this doctrine, that *in this fact lies our chief comfort.* In our hour of trouble, in our time of warfare, let us say, "Father." You notice that the first cry from the cross is like the last; the highest note is like the lowest. Jesus begins with, "Father, forgive them," and he finishes with, "Father, into thy hands I commend my spirit." To help you in a stern duty like forgiveness, cry, "Father." To help you in sore suffering and death, cry, "Father." Your main strength lies in your being truly a child of God.

Learn the next doctrine, that *dying is going home to our Father.* I said to an old friend, not long ago, "Old Mr. So-and-so has gone home." I meant that he was dead. He said, "Yes, where else should he go?" I thought that was a wise question. Where else should we go? When we grow grey, and our day's work is done, where should we go but home? So, when Christ has said, "It is finished," his next word, of course, is "Father." He has finished his earthly course, and now he will go home to heaven. Just as a child runs to its mother's bosom when it is tired, and wants to fall asleep, so Christ says, "Father," ere he falls asleep in death.

Learn another doctrine, that if God is our Father, and we regard ourselves as going home when we die, because we go to him, then *he will receive us*. There is no hint that we can commit our spirit to God, and yet that God will not have us. Remember how Stephen, beneath a shower of stones, cried, "Lord Jesus, receive my spirit." Let us, however we may die, make this our last emotion if not our last expression, "Father, receive my spirit." Shall not our heavenly Father receive his children? If ye, being evil, receive your children at nightfall, when they come home to sleep, shall not your Father, who is in heaven, receive you when your day's work is done? That is the doctrine we are to learn from this last cry from the cross, the Fatherhood of God and all that comes of it to believers.

II. Secondly, LET US PRACTISE THE DUTY.

That duty seems to me to be, first, *resignation*. Whenever anything distresses and alarms you, resign yourself to God. Say, "Father, into thy hands I commend my spirit." Sing with Faber,—

> "I bow me to thy will, O God,
>   And all thy ways adore;
>   And every day I live I'll seek
>   To please thee more and more."

Learn, next, the duty of *prayer*. When thou art in the very anguish of pain, when thou art surrounded by bitter griefs of mind as well as of body, still pray. Drop not the "Our Father." Let not your cries be addressed to the air; let not your moans be to your physician, or your nurse; but cry, "Father." Does not a child so cry when it has lost its way? If it be in the dark at night, and it starts up in a lone room, does it not cry out, "Father"; and is not a father's heart touched by that cry? Is there anybody here who has never cried to God? Is there one here who has never said "Father"? Then, my Father, put thy love into their hearts, and make them to-night say, "I will arise, and go to my Father." You shall truly be known to be the sons of God if that cry is in your heart and on your lips.

The next duty is *the committal of ourselves to God by faith*. Give yourselves up to God, trust yourselves with God. Every morning, when you get up, take yourself, and put yourself into God's custody; lock yourself up, as it were, in the casket of divine protection; and every night, when you have unlocked the box, ere you fall asleep, lock it again, and give the key into the hand of him who is able to keep you when the image of death is on your face. Before you sleep, commit yourself to God; I mean, do that when there is nothing to frighten you, when everything is going smoothly, when the wind blows softly from the south, and the barque is speeding towards its desired haven, still make not thyself quiet with thine own quieting.

He who carves for himself will cut his fingers, and get an empty
plate. He who leaves God to carve for him shall often have fat things
full of marrow placed before him. If thou canst trust, God will
reward thy trusting in a way that thou knowest not as yet.

And then practise one other duty, that of *the personal and continual*
realization of God's presence. " Father, into thy hands I commend my
spirit." " Thou art here; I know that thou art. I realize that thou
art here in the time of sorrow, and of danger; and I put myself into
thy hands. Just as I would give myself to the protection of a
policeman, or a soldier, if anyone attacked me, so do I commit myself
to thee, thou unseen Guardian of the night, thou unwearied Keeper of
the day. Thou shalt cover my head in the day of battle. Beneath
thy wings will I trust, as a chick hides beneath the hen."

See, then, your duty. It is to resign yourself to God, pray to God,
commit yourself to God, and rest in a sense of the presence of God.
May the Spirit of God help you in the practice of such priceless duties
as these!

III. Now, lastly, LET US ENJOY THE PRIVILEGE.

First, let us enjoy the high privilege of *resting in God in all times of*
danger and pain. The doctor has just told you that you will have to
undergo an operation. Say, " Father, into thy hands I commend my
spirit." There is every probability that that weakness of yours, or
that disease of yours, will increase upon you, and that by-and-by you
will have to take to your bed, and lie there perhaps for many a day.
Then say, " Father, into thy hands I commend my spirit." Do not
fret; for that will not help you. Do not fear the future; for that
will not aid you. Give yourself up (it is your privilege to do so) to
the keeping of those dear hands that were pierced for you, to the love
of that dear heart which was set abroach with the spear to purchase
your redemption. It is wonderful what rest of spirit God can give to
a man or a woman in the very worst condition. Oh, how some of the
martyrs have sung at the stake! How they have rejoiced when on
the rack! Bonner's coal-hole, across the water there, at Fulham,
where he shut up the martyrs, was a wretched place to lie in on a
cold winter's night; but they said, " They did rouse them in the straw,
as they lay in the coal-hole; with the sweetest singing out of heaven,
and when Bonner said, ' Fie on them that they should make such a
noise!' they told him that he, too, would make such a noise if he was
as happy as they were." When you have commended your spirit to
God, then you have sweet rest in time of danger and pain.

The next privilege is that of *a brave confidence, in the time of death,*
or in the fear of death. I was led to think over this text by using it a
great many times last Thursday night. Perhaps none of you will
ever forget last Thursday night. I do not think that I ever shall, if
I live to be as old as Methuselah. From this place till I reached my
home, it seemed one continued sheet of fire; and the further I went,
the more vivid became the lightning flashes; but when I came at last
to turn up Leigham Court Road, then the lightning seemed to come
in very bars from the sky; and at last, as I reached the top of the
hill, and a crash came of the most startling kind, down poured a
torrent of hail, hailstones that I will not attempt to describe, for you

might think that I exaggerated, and then I felt, and my friend with me, that we could hardly expect to reach home alive. We were there at the very centre and summit of the storm. All around us, on every side, and all within us, as it were, seemed nothing but the electric fluid; and God's right arm seemed bared for war. I felt then, "Well, now I am very likely going home," and I commended my spirit to God; and from that moment, though I cannot say that I took much pleasure in the peals of thunder, and the flashes of lightning, yet I felt quite as calm as I do here at this present moment; perhaps a little more calm than I do in the presence of so many people; happy at the thought that, within a single moment, I might understand more than all I could ever learn on earth, and see in an instant more than I could hope to see if I lived here for a century. I could only say to my friend, "Let us commit ourselves to God; we know that we are doing our duty in going on as we are going, and all is well with us." So we could only rejoice together in the prospect of being soon with God. We were not taken home in the chariot of fire; we are still spared a little longer to go on with life's work; but I realize the sweetness of being able to have done with it all, to have no wish, no will, no word, scarcely a prayer, but just to take one's heart up, and hand it over to the great Keeper, saying, "Father, take care of me. So let me live, so let me die. I have henceforth no desire about anything; let it be as *thou* pleasest. Into thy hands I commend my spirit."

This privilege is not only that of having rest in danger, and confidence in the prospect of death; it is also full of *consummate joy*. Beloved, if we know how to commit ourselves into the hands of God, what a place it is for us to be in! What a place to be in,—in the hands of God! There are the myriads of stars; there is the universe itself; God's hand upholds its everlasting pillars, and they do not fall. If we get into the hands of God, we get where all things rest, and we get home and happiness. We have got out of the nothingness of the creature into the all-sufficiency of the Creator. Oh, get you there; hasten to get you there, beloved friends, and live henceforth in the hands of God!

"It is finished." You have not finished; but Christ has. It is all done. What you have to do will only be to work out what he has already finished for you, and show it to the sons of men in your lives. And because it is all finished, therefore say, "Now, Father, I return to thee. My life henceforth shall be to be in thee. My joy shall be to shrink to nothing in the presence of the All-in-all, to die into the eternal life, to sink my *ego* into Jehovah, to let my manhood, my creaturehood live only for its Creator, and manifest only the Creator's glory. O beloved, begin to-morrow morning and end to-night with, "Father, into thy hands I commend my spirit." The Lord be with you all! Oh, if you have never prayed, God help you to begin to pray now, for Jesus' sake! Amen.

51—53. *And, behold, the veil of the temple was rent in twain from the top to the bottom; and the earth did quake, and the rocks rent; and the graves were opened; and many bodies of the saints which slept arose, and came out of the graves after his resurrection, and went into the holy city, and appeared unto many.*

Christ's death was the end of Judaism: *The veil of the temple was rent in twain from the top to the bottom.* As if shocked at the sacrilegious murder of her Lord, the temple rent her garments, like one stricken with horror at some stupendous crime. The body of Christ being rent, the veil of the temple was torn in twain from the top to the bottom. Now was there an entrance made into the holiest of all, by the blood of Jesus; and a way of access to God was opened for every sinner who trusted in Christ's atoning sacrifice.

See what marvels accompanied and followed the death of Christ: *The earth did quake, and the rocks rent; and the graves were opened.* Thus did the material world pay homage to him whom man had rejected; while nature's convulsions foretold what will happen when Christ's voice once more shakes not the earth only, but also heaven.

These first miracles wrought in connection with the death of Christ were typical of spiritual wonders that will be continued till he comes again,—rocky hearts are rent, graves of sin are opened, those who have been dead in trespasses and sins, and buried in sepulchres of lust and evil, are quickened, and come out from among the dead, and go unto *the holy city*, the New Jerusalem.

54. *Now when the centurion, and they that were with him, watching Jesus, saw the earthquake, and those things that were done, they feared greatly, saying, Truly this was the Son of God.*

These Roman soldiers had never witnessed such scenes in connection with an execution before, and they could only come to one conclusion about the illustrious prisoner whom they had put to death: " *Truly this was the Son of God.*" It was strange that those men should confess what the chief priests and scribes and elders denied; yet since their day it has often happened that the most abandoned and profane have acknowledged Jesus as the Son of God while their religious rulers have denied his divinity.

10. The Miracles
of Our Lord's Death

"Jesus, when he had cried again with a loud voice, yielded up the ghost. And, behold, the veil of the temple was rent in twain from the top to the bottom; and the earth did quake, and the rocks rent; and the graves were opened; and many bodies of the saints which slept arose, and came out of the graves after his resurrection, and went into the holy city, and appeared unto many."—Matthew xxvii. 50—53.

OUR Lord's death is a marvel set in a surrounding of marvels. It reminds one of a Kohinoor surrounded with a circle of gems. As the sun, in the midst of the planets which surround it, far outshines them all, so the death of Christ is more wonderful than the miracles which happened at the time. Yet, after having seen the sun, we take a pleasure in studying the planets, and so, after believing in the unique death of Christ, and putting our trust in him as the Crucified One, we find it a great pleasure to examine in detail those four planetary wonders mentioned in the text, which circle round the great sun of the death of our Lord himself.

Here they are: *the veil of the temple was rent in twain; the earth did quake; the rocks rent; the graves were opened.*

I. To begin with the first of these wonders. I cannot, to-night, enlarge. I have not the strength. I wish merely to suggest thoughts.

Consider THE RENT VEIL, or *mysteries laid open.* By the death of Christ the veil of the temple was rent in twain from the top to the bottom, and the mysteries which had been concealed in the most holy place throughout many generations were laid open to the gaze of all believers. Beginning, as it were, at the top in the Deity of Christ, down to the lowest part of Christ's manhood, the veil was rent, and everything was discovered to every spiritual eye.

1. *This was the first miracle of Christ after death.* The first miracle of Christ in life was significant, and taught us much. He turned the water into wine, as if to show that he raised all common life to a

higher grade, and put into all truth a power and a sweetness, which could not have been there apart from him. But this first miracle of his after death stands above the first miracle of his life, because, if you will remember, that miracle was wrought in his presence. He was there, and turned the water into wine. But Jesus, as man, was not in the temple. That miracle was wrought in his absence, and it enhances its wonder. They are both equally miraculous, but there is a touch more striking about this second miracle—that he was not there to speak and make the veil rend in twain. His soul had gone from his body, and neither his body nor his soul was in that secret place of the tabernacles of the Most High; and yet, at a distance, his will sufficed to rend that thick veil of fine twined linen and cunning work.

The miracle of turning water into wine was wrought in a private house, amidst the family and such disciples as were friends of the family; but this marvel was wrought in the temple of God. There is a singular sacredness about it, because it was a deed of wonder done in that most awful and mysterious place, which was the centre of hallowed worship, and the abode of God. See! he dies, and at the very door of God's high sanctuary he rends the veil in twain. There is a solemnity about this miracle, as wrought before Jehovah, which I can hardly convey in speech, but which you will feel in your own souls.

Do not forget also that this was done by the Saviour after his death, and this sets the miracle in a very remarkable light. He rends the veil at the very instant of death. Jesus yielded up the ghost, and, behold, the veil of the temple was rent in twain. For thirty years he seems to have prepared himself for the first miracle of his life; he works his first miracle after death in the moment of expiring. As his soul departed from his body our blessed Lord at that same moment laid hold upon the great veil of his Father's symbolical house, and rent it in twain.

2. This first miracle after death stands in such a place that we cannot pass it by without grave thought. *It was very significant, as standing at the head of what I may call a new dispensation.* The miracle of turning water into wine begins his public life, and sets the key of it. This begins his **work** after death, and marks the tone of it. What does it mean?

Does it not mean that *the death of Christ is the revelation and explanation of secrets?* Vanish all the types and shadows of the ceremonial law;—vanish because fulfilled and explained in the death of Christ. The death of the Lord Jesus is the key of all true philosophy: God made flesh, dying for man—if that does not explain a mystery, it cannot be explained. If with this thread in your hand you cannot follow the labyrinth of human affairs, and learn the great purpose of God, then you cannot follow it at all. The death of Christ is the great veil-render, the great revealer of secrets.

It is also the great opener of entrances. There was no way into the holy place till Jesus, dying, rent the veil; the way into the most holy of all was not made manifest till he died. If you desire to approach God, the death of Christ is the way to him. If you want the nearest access and the closest communion that a creature can have with his God, behold, the sacrifice of Christ reveals the way to you. Jesus not only says, "I am the way," but, rending the veil, he makes the way. The veil of his flesh being rent, the way to God is made most clear to every believing soul.

Moreover, *the cross is the clearing of all obstacles.* Christ by death rent the veil. Then between his people and heaven there remains no obstruction, or if there be any—if your fears invent an obstruction—the Christ who rent the veil continues still to rend it. He breaks the gates of brass, and cuts the bars of iron in sunder. Behold, in his death "the breaker is come up before them, and the Lord on the head of them." He has broken up and cleared the way, and all his chosen people may follow him up to the glorious throne of God.

This is significant of the spirit of the dispensation under which we now live. Obstacles are cleared; difficulties are solved; heaven is opened to all believers.

3. *It was a miracle worthy of Christ.* Stop a minute and adore your dying Lord. Does he with such a miracle signalize his death? Does it not prove his *immortality?* It is true he has bowed his head in death. Obedient to his Father's will, when he knows that the time has come for him to die, he bows his head in willing acquiescence; but at that moment when you call him dead, he rends the veil of the temple. Is there not immortality in him though he died?

And see what *power* he possessed. His hands are nailed; his side is about to be pierced. As he hangs there he cannot protect himself from the insults of the soldiery, but in his utmost weakness he is so strong that he rends the heavy veil of the temple from the top to the bottom.

Behold his *wisdom,* for in this moment, viewing the deed spiritually, he opens up to us all wisdom, and lays bare the secrets of God. The veil which Moses put upon his face Christ takes away in the moment of his death. The true Wisdom in his dying preaches his grandest sermon by tearing away that which hid the supremest truth from the gaze of all believing eyes.

Beloved, if Jesus does this for us in his death, surely, we shall be saved by his life. Jesus who died is yet alive, and we trust in him to lead us into "the holy places made without hands."

Before I pass on to the second wonder, I invite everyone here, who as yet does not know the Saviour, seriously to think upon the miracles which attended his death, and judge what sort of man he was who, for our sins, thus laid down his life. He was not suffered by the Father to die without a miracle to show that he had made a way for sinners to draw near to God.

II. Pass on now to the second wonder—"THE EARTH DID QUAKE." *The immovable was stirred by the death of Christ.* Christ did not touch the earth: he was uplifted from it on the tree. He was dying, but in the laying aside of his power, in the act of death, he made the earth beneath him, which we call "the solid globe," itself to quake. What did it teach?

Did it not mean, first, *the physical universe fore-feeling the last terrible shake of its doom?* The day will come when the Christ will appear upon the earth, and in due time all things that are shall be rolled up, like garments worn out, and put away. Once more will he speak, and then will he shake not only the earth, but also heaven. The things which cannot be shaken will remain, but this earth is not one of them: it will be shaken out of its place. "The earth also and the works that are therein shall be burned up." Nothing shall stand before him. He alone is. These other things do but seem to be; and before the terror of his face all men shall tremble, and heaven and earth shall flee away. So, when he died, earth seemed to anticipate its doom, and quaked in his presence. How will it quake when he that lives again shall come with all the glory of God! How will you quake, my hearer, if you should wake up in the next world without a Saviour! How will you tremble in that day when he shall come to judge the world in righteousness, and you shall have to face the Saviour whom you have despised! Think of it, I pray you.

Did not that miracle also mean this?—that *the spiritual world is to be moved by the cross of Christ.* He dies upon the cross and shakes the material world, as a prediction that that death of his would shake the world that lieth in the wicked one, and cause convulsions in the moral kingdom. Brothers, think of it. We say of ourselves, "How shall we ever move the world?" The apostles did not ask that question. They had confidence in the gospel which they preached. Those who heard them saw that confidence; and when they opened their mouths they said, "The men that have turned the world upside down have come hither unto us." The apostles believed in shaking the world with the simple preaching of the gospel. I entreat you to believe the same. It is a vast city this—this London. How can we ever affect it? China, Hindostan, Africa—these are immense regions. Will the cross of Christ tell upon them? Yes, my brethren, for it shook the earth, and it will yet shake the great masses of mankind. If we have but faith in it, and perseverance to keep on with the preaching of the Word, it is but a matter of time when the name of Jesus shall be known of all men, and when every knee shall bow to him, and every tongue confess that he is Christ, to the glory of God the Father. The earth did quake beneath the cross; and it shall again. The Lord God be praised for it.

That old world—how many years it had existed I cannot tell. The age of the world, from that beginning which is mentioned in the first verse of the Book of Genesis, we are not able to compute. However old it was, it had to shake when the Redeemer died. This carries us over another of our difficulties. The system of evil we have to deal with is so long-established, hoary, and reverent with antiquity, that we say to ourselves, "We cannot do much against old prejudices." But it was the old, old earth that quivered and quaked beneath the dying Christ, and it shall do so again. Magnificent systems, sustained by philosophy and poetry, will yet yield before what is called the comparatively new doctrine of the cross. Assuredly it is not new, but older than the earth itself. It is God's own gospel, everlasting and eternal. It will shake down the antique and the venerable, as surely as the Lord liveth; and I see the prophecy of this in the quaking of the earth beneath the cross.

It does seem impossible, does it not, that the mere preaching of Christ can do this? And hence certain men must link to the preaching of Christ all the aids of music and architecture, and I know not what beside, till the cross of Christ is overlaid with human inventions, crushed and buried beneath the wisdom of man. But what was it that made the earth quake? Simply our Lord's death, and no addition of human power or wisdom. It seemed a very inadequate means to produce so great a result; but it was sufficient, for the "weakness of God is stronger than men, and the foolishness of God is wiser than men"; and Christ, in his very death, suffices to make the earth quake beneath his cross. Come, let us be well content in the battle in which we are engaged, to use no weapon but the gospel, no battle-axe but the cross. Could we but believe it the old, old story is the only story that is needed to be told to reconcile man to God. Jesus died in the sinner's stead, the just for the unjust, a magnificent display of God's grace and justice in one single act. Could we but keep to this only, we should see the victory coming speedily to our conquering Lord.

I leave that second miracle; wherein you see the immovable stirred in the quaking of the earth.

III. Only a hint or two upon the third miracle—THE ROCKS RENT.

I have been informed that, to this very day, there are at Jerusalem certain marks of rock-rending of the most unusual kind. Travellers have said that they are not such as are usually produced by earthquake, or any other cause. Upon that I will say but little; but it is a wonderful thing that, as Jesus died, as his soul was rent from his body, as the veil of the temple was rent in two, so the earth, the rocky part of it, the most solid structure of all, was rent in gulfs and chasms in a single moment. What does this miracle show us but this—*the insensible startled?* What! Could rocks feel? Yet they rent at the sight of Christ's death. Men's hearts did not respond to the agonizing cries of the dying Redeemer, but the rocks responded: the rocks were rent. He did not die for rocks; yet rocks were more tender than the hearts of men, for whom he shed his blood.

> "Of reason all things show some sign,
> But this unfeeling heart of mine,"

said the poet; and he spoke the truth. Rocks could rend, but yet some men's hearts are not rent by the sight of the cross. However, beloved, here is the point that I seem to see here—that obstinacy and *obduracy will be conquered* by the death of Christ. You may preach to a man about death, and he will not tremble at its certainty or solemnity; yet try him with it. You may preach to a man about hell, but he will harden his heart, like Pharaoh, against the judgment of the Lord; yet try him with it. All things that can move man should be used. But that which does affect the most obdurate and obstinate is the great love of God, so strangely seen in the death of the Lord Jesus Christ. I will not stay to show you how it is, but I will remind you that it is so. It was this which, in the case of many of us, brought tears of repentance to our eyes, and led us to submit to the will of God. I know that it was so with me. I looked at a thousand things, and I did not relent; but when

> "I saw One hanging on a tree
> In agonies and blood,"

and dying there for me, then did I smite upon my breast, and I was in bitterness for him, as one that is in bitterness for his first-born. I am sure your own hearts confess that the great rock-render is the dying Saviour.

Well, now, as it is with you, so shall you find it with other men. When you have done your best, and have not succeeded, bring out this last hammer—the cross of Christ. I have often seen on pieces of cannon, in Latin words, this inscription, "The last argument of kings." That is to say, cannons are the last argument of kings. But the cross is the last argument of God. If a dying Saviour does not convert you, what will? If his bleeding wounds do not attract you to God, what will? If Jesus bears our sin in his own body on the tree, and puts it away, and if this does not bring you to God, with confession of your sin, and hatred of it, then there remains nothing more for you. "How shall we escape if we neglect so great salvation?" The cross is the rock-render. Brothers and sisters, go on teaching the love of the dying Son of God. Go on preaching Christ. You will tunnel the Alps of pride and the granite hills of prejudice with this. You shall find an entrance for Christ into the inmost hearts of men, though they be hard as adamant; and this will be by the preaching of the cross in the power of the Spirit.

IV. But now I close with the last miracle. These wonders accumulate, and they depend upon each other. The quaking earth produced, no doubt, the rending of the rocks; and the rending of the rocks aided in the fourth wonder. "THE GRAVES WERE OPENED." The graves opened, and *the dead revived.* That is our fourth head. It is the great consequence of the death of Christ. The graves were opened. Man is the only animal that cares about a sepulchre. Some persons fret about how they shall be buried. That is the last concern that ever would cross my mind. I feel persuaded that people will bury me out of hatred, or out of love, and especially out of love to themselves. We need not trouble about that. But man has often shown his pride by his tomb. That is a strange thing. To garland the gallows is a novelty, I think, not yet perpetrated; but to pile marble and choice statuary upon a tomb—what is it but to adorn a gibbet, or to show man's great grandeur where his littleness is alone apparent. Dust, ashes, rottenness, putridity, and then a statue, and all manner of fine things, to make you think that the creature that goes back to dust is, after all, a great one. Now, when Jesus died, *sepulchres were laid bare, and the dead were exposed:* what does this mean?

I think we have in this last miracle "the history of a man." There he lies dead—corrupt, dead in trespasses and sins. But what a beautiful sepulchre he lies in! He is a church-goer; he is a dissenter —whichever you please of the two; he is a very moral person; he is a gentleman; he is a citizen; he is Master of his Company; he will be Lord Mayor one day; he is so good—oh, he is so good! yet he has no grace in his heart, no Christ in his faith, no love to God. You see what a sepulchre he lies in—a dead soul in a gilded tomb. By his cross our Lord splits this sepulchre and destroys it. What are our merits worth in the presence of the cross? The death of Christ is the death of self-righteousness. Jesus' death is a superfluity if we can save ourselves. If we are so good that we do not want the Saviour, why, then, did Jesus bleed his life away upon the tree? The cross breaks up the sepulchres of hypocrisy, formalism, and self-righteousness in which the spiritually dead are hidden away.

What next? *It opens the graves.* The earth springs apart. There lies the dead man: he is revealed to the light. The cross of Christ does that! The man is not yet made alive by grace, but he is discovered to himself. He knows that he lies in the grave of his sin. He has sufficient of the power of God upon him to make him lie, not like a corpse covered up with marble, but like a corpse from which the grave-digger has flung away the sods, and left it naked to the light of day. Oh, it is a grand thing when the cross thus opens the graves! You cannot convince men of sin except by the preaching of a crucified Saviour. The lance with which we reach the hearts of men is that same lance which pierced the Saviour's heart. We have to use the crucifixion as the means of crucifying self-righteousness, and making the man confess that he is dead in sin.

After the sepulchres had been broken up, and the graves had been opened, what followed next? *Life was imparted.* "Many of the bodies of the saints which slept arose." They had turned to dust; but when you have a miracle you may as well have a great one. I wonder that people, when they can believe one miracle, make any difficulty of another. Once introduce Omnipotence, and difficulties have ceased. So in this miracle. The bodies came together on a sudden, and there they were, complete and ready for the rising. What a wonderful thing is the implantation of life! I will not speak of it in a dead *man*, but I would speak of it in a dead *heart*. O God, send thy life into some dead heart at this moment while I speak! That which brings life into dead souls is the death of Jesus. While we behold the atonement, and view our Lord bleeding in our stead, the divine Spirit works upon the man, and life is breathed into him. He takes away the heart of stone, and gives a heart of flesh that palpitates with a new life. This is the wondrous work of the cross: it is by the death of our Lord that regeneration comes to men. There were no new births if it were not for that one death. If Jesus had not died, we had remained dead. If he had not bowed his head, none of us could have lifted up our heads. If he had not there on the cross passed from among the living, we must have remained among the dead for ever and for ever.

Now pass on, and you will see that those persons who received life, in due time *quitted their graves.* It is written that they came out of their graves. Of course they did. What living men would wish to stay in their graves? And you, my dear hearers, if the Lord quickens you, will not stay in your graves. If you have been accustomed to strong drink, or to any other besetting sin, you will quit it; you will not feel any attachment to your sepulchre. If you have lived in ungodly company, and found amusement in questionable places, you will not stop in your graves. We shall not have need to come after you to lead you away from your old associations. You will be eager to get out of them. If any person here should be buried alive, and if he should be discovered in his coffin before he had breathed his last, I am sure that, if the sod were lifted, and the lid were taken off, he would not need prayerful entreaties to come out of his grave. Far from it. Life loves not the prison of death. So may God grant that the dying Saviour may fetch you out of the graves in which you are still living; and, if he now quickens you, I am sure that the death of our Lord will make you reckon that if one died for all, then all died, and that he died for all, that they which live should not live henceforth unto themselves, but unto him that died for them and rose again.

Which way did these people go after they had come out of their graves? We are told that "*they went into the holy city.*" Exactly so. And he that has felt the power of the cross may well make the best of his way to holiness. He will long to join himself with God's people; he will wish to go up to God's house, and to have fellowship with the thrice-holy God. I should not expect that quickened ones would go anywhere else. Every creature goes to its own company, the beast to its lair, and the bird to its nest; and the restored and regenerated man makes his way to the holy city. Does not the cross draw us to the church of God? I would not wish one to join the church from any motive that is not fetched from the five wounds and bleeding side of Jesus. We give ourselves first to Christ, and then to his people for his dear sake. It is the cross that does it

> ※ Jesus dead upon the tree
> Achieves this wondrous victory."

We are told—to close this marvellous story—that they went into the Holy City "*and appeared unto many.*" That is, some of them who had been raised from the dead, I do not doubt, appeared unto their wives. What rapture as they saw again the beloved husband! It may be that some of them appeared to father and mother; and I doubt not that many a quickened mother or father would make the first appearance to their children. What does this teach us, but that, if the Lord's grace should raise us from the dead, we must take care to show it? Let us appear unto many. Let the life that God has given us be manifest. Let us not hide it, but let us go to our former friends and make our epiphanies as Christ made his. For his glory's sake let us have our manifestation and appearance unto others. Glory be to the dying Saviour! All praise to the great Sacrifice!

Oh, that these poor, feeble words of mine would excite some interest in you about my dying Master! Be ready to die for him. And you that do not know him—think of this great mystery—that God should take your nature and become a man and die, that you might not die, and bear your sin that you should be free from it. Come and trust my Lord to-night, I pray you. While the people of God gather at the table to the breaking of bread, let your spirits hasten, not to the table and the sacrament, but to Christ himself and his sacrifice. Amen.

11. The Messages
of Our Lord's Love

"Go your way, tell his disciples and Peter that he goeth before you into Galilee: there shall ye see him, as he said unto you."—Mark xvi. 7.

SEE, brethren! Jesus delights to meet his people. He is no sooner risen from the dead than he sends a message by an angel to say that he will meet his disciples. His delight is in them. He loves them with a very tender love, and he is happiest when he is in their midst. Do not think that you will have to entreat and persuade your Lord to come to you; he delights in near and dear fellowship. The heavenly Bridegroom finds solace in your company, if you be indeed espoused to him. Oh, that you were more anxious to be with him!

Our Lord knows that, to his true people, the greatest joy they ever have is for him to meet them. The disciples were at their saddest. Their Lord, as they thought, was dead. They had just passed the dreariest Sabbath of their lives, for he was in the tomb; and now, to comfort them, he sends no message but this—that he will meet them. He knew that there would be magic in that news to cheer their aching hearts. *He would meet them:* that would be all-sufficient consolation: "Go into Galilee; there shall ye see *him*."

If all the sorrows of God's people could be poured out in one vast pile, what a mountain they would make! How varied our distresses! How diverse our depressions! But, beloved, if Jesus will meet us, all the sadness will fly away, and all the sorrow will grow light. Only give us his company, and we have all things. You know what I mean, many of you. Our Lord has made our hearts to leap for joy in sorrowful times. When we have been filled with physical pain, his company has made us forget the body's weakness; and when we have newly come from the grave, and our heart has been ready to break through bereavement, the sight of the Saviour has sweetened our bitter cup. In his presence we have felt resigned to the great Father's will, and content to say, "It is the Lord: let him do what seemeth him good." Until the day break, and the shadows flee away for ever, we want nothing but our Well-beloved's company. "Abide with me! Abide with me!"—this is our one prayer; and if we have that fulfilled, all other desires may wait their turn.

My subject is chosen with a view to our coming, as we always do on the first day of the week, to this table of communion. I want every child of God here to seek after, nay, to gain, full fellowship with Christ. I long to enjoy it myself, that I may preach a Saviour in whose presence I live. I long for you to enjoy it, that you may hear, not my voice, but his voice, which is sweeter than the music of angels' harps. Oh, that those who do not know our Lord may now be set a-hungering after his surpassing sweetness! He is willing to come to you. A prayer will find him; a tear will draw him; a look of faith will hold him fast. Cast yourself on Jesus, and his open arms will joyously receive you.

But now to the text. I shall take it just as it stands, and make five observations upon it.

I. The first is: JESUS, THAT HE MAY MEET HIS PEOPLE, ISSUES INVITATIONS, AND THE INVITATIONS ARE VERY GRACIOUS—"Go, tell his disciples and Peter." "*Tell his disciples.*" The invitation is most gracious as directed to them, for "they all forsook him, and fled." On that night, that doleful night, when he most needed company, they slept; and when he woke, and was taken off to the hall of Caiaphas, they fled—yes, every one of them; there was not a steadfast spirit among them. They all fled. "Shame on them!" say you? Yes, but Jesus was not ashamed of them; for in one of the first speeches of his glorious life on earth he specially mentions them. "Tell my disciples": not picking and choosing, here and there, a heart more faithful than the rest, but mentioning the whole coward company, he says, "Tell my disciples." Brethren, disciples of Christ, Jesus would meet us now; let us hasten to his presence. Not one among us dares plume himself upon his fidelity; we have all at times played the coward. We may each one of us hide our faces when we think of our Lord's most faithful love to us. We have never acted towards him according to his deserts. If he had banished us: if he had said, "I will no more acknowledge this dastard company," we could not have wondered; but he invites us all, all who are his disciples—invites us to himself. Will you stay away? Will any of you be satisfied without beholding that dear countenance, more marred than that of any man, and yet more lovely than the face of angels? Come ye, all who follow him, for he bids you come. Hear the address of the message—"Tell my disciples."

But the bounty and beauty of his grace lay in this—that one had been worse than the rest, and, therefore, for him there is a special finger to beckon him, a special word to call him: "Tell my disciples AND PETER." He that denied his Lord, he that cursed as he denied, he who, after boisterous self-confidence, trembled at the jest of a maid, is he to be called? Yes, "Tell my disciples *and Peter.*" If any of you have behaved worse to your Master than others, you are peculiarly called to come to him now. You have grieved him, and you have been grieving because you have grieved him. You have been brought to repentance after having slidden away from him, and now he seals your pardon by inviting you to himself. He bids you not to stand in the background, but to come in with the rest and commune with him.

Peter, where art thou? The crowing of the cock is still in thine ear, and the tear is still in thine eye, yet come and welcome, for thou lovest him. He knows thou dost. Thou art grieved that a doubt should be put upon thy love. Come, he has forgiven thee; he has given thee tokens of it in thy broken heart and tearful eye. Come, Peter! Come thou, if nobody else should come. Jesus Christ invites thee by name before any other. In this place may be believers who have acted strangely, and have even forsaken the Lord, and they are now bemoaning themselves. Go on with your holy sorrow, but come to your Lord. Be not content till you have seen him, till you have laid hold upon him by a fresh grip of faith, and till you can say, "My beloved is mine, and I am his."

Most tender, then, are the invitations which Jesus issues. Part of the tenderness now lies in *the lips which deliver the message* on the Lord's behalf. The women came, and said—Jesus has said to us, by an angel, he will go before us into Galilee, and there shall ye see him. I am always thankful that God has committed the ministry of the Word, not to angels, but to us poor men. As I told you a little while ago, you may grow tired of me and my stammerings; but yet they are more suitable for you than nobler strains might be. I have no doubt that if you had an angel to preach to you, there would be a very great crowd, and for a time you would say, "It is wonderful"; but it would be so cold from lack of human sympathy, that you would soon weary of the lofty style. An angel would try to be kind, as became his heavenly nature, but he would not be *kinned*, and you must necessarily miss the kindness which comes of kinship. I speak to you as bone of your bone, and flesh of your flesh: I speak to you, teacher, for I am a teacher. I speak to you, disciple, for I am a disciple, and I dare not think myself greater than the least of you. Let us come hand in hand to our dear Saviour, and all together let us pray him to manifest himself to us as he doth not unto the world. This, then, is my first point—his invitations are gracious.

II. Secondly, we see in our text that JESUS KEEPS HIS TRYST. "I will go before you into Galilee." If you turn to Mark xiv. 27, 28, you will see that he told them before he died, "All ye shall be offended because of me this night: for it is written, I will smite the shepherd, and the sheep shall be scattered. But after that I am risen, I will go before you into Galilee." He will be where he says he will be. Jesus never breaks a promise. It is a great vexation, especially to us who are very busy, when somebody says, "Will you meet me at such and such a place?" "Yes; at what hour?" The hour is appointed. We are there. Thank God, we never were a half minute behind time when it was possible to be punctual; but punctuality is a lesson which very few persons as yet have learned. We wait, and wait wearily, and perhaps we leave the place to let our dilatory friends know that if they are in eternity we are in time, and cannot afford to lose any of it. Many people make an engagement and break it, as if it were just nothing at all to be guilty of a practical lie. It is not so with Jesus: he says, "I will go before you into Galilee"; and into Galilee he will go.

When he promises to meet his people he will meet with them without fail, and without delay.

Let us dwell on this appointment for a minute. Why did our Lord say that he would go to Galilee? Was it because *it was his old haunt*, and being risen from the dead, he desired to go back to the spot where he had been accustomed to be—to the lake, and to the hillside? Surely there is something in that. It was *their* old haunt, too: they were fishermen on that lake, and he would take them back to the place where a thousand memories would be awakened by their voices, like echoes which lie asleep among the hills. Besides it would provide witnesses to his identity, for the Galileans knew him well: since there he had been brought up. He would go where he was known, and show himself in his former places of resort.

Perhaps, too, it was because *the place was despised*. He has risen, and he will go to Galilee. He is not ashamed to be called the Galilean and the Nazarene. The risen One does not go to the halls of princes, but to the villages of peasants and fishermen. There was no pride in Jesus: not even the smell of that fire had passed upon him. He was ever meek and lowly in heart.

Did he not also go to Galilee, because *it was some little distance* from Jerusalem, that those who would meet him might take a little trouble? Our Beloved would be sought after. A journey after him will endear his society. He will not meet you at Jerusalem, perhaps— at least, not the whole company of you; but he will show himself by the sea in distant Galilee.

Do you think he went to Galilee because *it was " Galilee of the Gentiles*," that he might get as near to us Gentiles as his mission allowed? He was sent as a preacher only to the lost sheep of the house of Israel; but he travelled to the very edge of his diocese to get as near to the Gentiles (I mean to ourselves) as he could. Oh, happy word for us aliens!—"I will go before you into Galilee." So he said; and when he left the tomb, he kept his word.

Now, beloved, we have his word for it, that he will come and meet us where we are met together. "Where two or three are gathered together in my name, there am I in the midst of them"; and does he not keep his word? How many times in our assemblies, great and small, have we said, "The Lord was there"! How frequently have we forgotten preacher and fellow-worshippers, feeling ourselves in the presence of a greater than mortal man! Our eyes of faith have seen the King in his beauty, revealing his love to us. Oh, yes! he keeps his tryst. He comes to his people, and he never disappoints them. I think this is particularly true of the table of communion. How often he has met us there! I am compelled to repeat my personal testimony. I have never omitted being at the Lord's table on any Sabbath of my life for many years past, except when I have been ill, or unable to attend; and I am therefore able to answer the question—Does not frequency diminish the solemnity of the ordinance? I have not found it so; but the rather it grows upon me. That broken bread, that poured out wine, the emblems of his flesh and blood—these bring him very near. It seems as if sense lent aid to faith; and through these two windows of agates, and gates of carbuncles, we come very near to our

Lord. What have we here but himself, under instructive emblems? What do we here but remember him? What is our business here but to show his death until he come? And so, though we may not have seen him in converse by the way, for our eyes have been holden, yet we have seen him in the breaking of bread. May it be always so! May we prove that Jesus keeps his pledge. He will be with us even now. Suppose Jesus had said that he would come into this place to-night in literal flesh and blood, you would be all sitting in expectation, and saying to each other, "When will he come?" The preacher would be waiting to drop back, or fall upon his knees in adoration, while his Master stood in the front. You will not see him *so;* but may your faith, which is much better than eyesight, realize him as the present Christ, near to each one of you. If he were here in the flesh, he might stand *here,* and then he might be near to me, but far off from my friends yonder; but coming in spirit he can be equally near to us all, and speak to each one of us personally, as though each one were the only person present.

III. My third observation is, JESUS IS ALWAYS FIRST AT EVERY APPOINTED MEETING. So runs the text: *"He goeth before you* into Galilee." Remember that promise, "Where two or three are gathered together in my name, there *am* I"—not "there will I be." Jesus is there before his disciples reach the place. The first to reach the house is he who is first in the house. We come to him: it is not that we meet, and then he comes to us; but he goes before us, and we gather to him.

Does it not teach us that *he is the shepherd?* He said, "Smite the shepherd, and the sheep shall be scattered; but after I am risen, I will go before you into Galilee." He would take up the shepherd's place again, and go before the flock, and the sheep would take up the position of the flock again, no longer scattered, but following at the Shepherd's heel. Great Master, come to-night; call thy sheep to thyself! Speak to us, look upon us, and we will arise, and follow thee.

Is he not first, next, because *he is the centre?* We gather to him. You must choose a centre before you can mark the circumference. When Israel travelled through the wilderness, the first place to pitch upon for an encampment was the place where the tabernacle and the ark should rest, and then the tents were set around it. Jesus is our centre; he must therefore be first, and we rejoice to hear him say, "I will go before you into Galilee." He will take the first place, and we will cluster about him as bees around their queen. Do you always gather to the name of Christ, beloved? If you gather to the name of any minister, or any sect, you gather amiss. Our gatherings must be unto the Lord Jesus: he must be the centre, and he alone; let us take care of that.

Next, he goes before us naturally, because *he is the host.* If there is to be a feast, the first person to be there is the one who provides it —the master or mistress who sits at the head of the table. It would never do for the guests to be there first, and then for the master to come hurrying home, crying, "Excuse me: I quite forgot that you were to be here at six o'clock!" Oh no, the host must be first! When Jesus bids us come to him, and says he will sup with us, and we with him, he will be sure to be first, so as to prepare the feast. He goes before us into Galilee.

But surely, the reason why he is first is this—that *he is more ready for us than we are for him.* It takes us time to get ready for communion, to dress our souls, and collect our thoughts. Are you all ready for the Lord's Supper to-night? Some of you, perhaps, have come carelessly here, and yet you are members of the church, and mean to stay to the Supper. Beloved, try to come with a prepared heart, for the communion will be to you very much what you make it; and if your thoughts and desires are not right, what can the outward emblems be to you? On our Lord's part all things are ready, and he waits to receive you, and to bless you. Therefore he is first at the appointed meeting-place.

I may also add that *he is much more eager to have fellowship with you than you are to have fellowship with him.* It is a strange thing that it should be so, but so it is. He, the great lover of our souls, burns with a passionate desire to press his people to his heart; and we, the objects of such a matchless love, start back, and reward the ardour of his affection with lukewarmness. It must not be so on this occasion. I have said to my Lord, "Let me either feast upon thee or hunger after thee." I pray that you may have such a burning thirst for Jesus at this hour that you *must* drink of his cup or pine with thirst for him.

IV. The fourth observation is this: THE LORD JESUS REVEALS HIMSELF TO HIS PEOPLE. How does the text run? "He goeth before you into Galilee. *There shall ye see him.*" The main object is to *see him.* He will go to Galilee on purpose that he may reveal himself to them. My dear brethren, this is what they needed beyond all else. Their sorrow was because they thought him dead; their joy would be because they saw him alive. Their griefs were multiform, but this one consolation would end them all. If they could but see Jesus, they would look their fears away. What have you come here for to-night, children of God? I trust that you can answer, "Sir, we would see Jesus." If our Master will come, and we shall feel his presence, it will not matter how feebly I speak, or how poor the service may be in itself; you will say, "It was good to be there, for the Lord drew near to us in all the glory of his love." *His presence is what you want.*

And *this is what he readily gives.* Jesus is very familiar with his people. Some worship a Saviour who sits enthroned above in the stately dignity of indifference; but our Lord is not so. Though reigning in heaven, he is still conversant with his people below. He is a brother born for adversity. Spiritually he communes with us. Do you know what the company of Christ is? Are you altogether taken up with doctrines about him, or with ceremonies that concern him? If so, yours is a poor life; but the joy of the inner life is to know, and to speak with, and to dwell with the Lord Jesus. Do you understand this? I charge you, be not satisfied till you come to personal and intimate intercourse with your Lord. Short of this, you are short of the privilege which he sees you need, for this is his great promise, "There shall ye see me."

What is more, this sight of him *is what our Lord effectually bestows.* Jesus not only exhibits himself, but he opens our eyes, that we may enjoy the sight. "There *shall* ye see me." He may be manifest, and yet blind eyes will not see him. Blessed Master, come and take the scales away and make our hearts capable of spiritual perception! It is not everybody that can see God, and yet God is everywhere. The eye must first be cleansed. Jesus says, "There shall ye see me"; and he knows how to open our eyes, so that we do see him. Our Lord can make this to be the absorbing occupation of his people. "He goeth before you into Galilee"—and what then? "There shall ye see him." Why, they went fishing, did they not? Yes, but they were called off from that. "There shall ye see him." They took a great haul of fish, did they not? Yes, yes, yes; but that was a mere incident: the grand fact was, that they *saw him.* I pray the Lord to make the one occupation of our lives the seeing of HIM. May all the lower lights grow dim. Where are the stars at midday? They are all in their places, but you only see the sun. Where are a thousand things when Christ appears? They are all where they should be, but you only see *him.* May the Lord cause all other loves to vanish, and himself alone to fill our hearts, so that it may be true of us, "There shall ye see him"!

I have thus far proceeded, crying to the Holy Ghost for help, and now comes the fifth observation, with which we close.

V. OUR LORD REMEMBERS HIS OWN PROMISES. It was before he died that he said he would go before them into Galilee, and now that he has risen from the dead, he says, by the mouth of his angel, "There shall ye see him, *as he said unto you.*" The rule of Christ's action is his own word. What he has said he will perform. You and I forget his promises, but *he* never does. "As he said unto you" is the remembrance of all that he has spoken. Why does our Lord remember and repeat what he has so graciously spoken?

He does so because *he spoke with foresight,* and forethought, and care. We make promises and forget them because we did not consider well the matter before we spoke; but if we have thought, calculated, weighed, estimated, and come to a deliberate resolve before we speak, then we earnestly remember what we resolved upon. No promise of our Lord Jesus has been spoken in haste, to be repented of afterwards. Infinite wisdom directs infinite love; and when infinite love takes the pen to write a promise, infallible wisdom dictates every syllable.

Jesus does not forget, because *he spoke the promise with his whole heart.* It is not every tongue that represents a heart at all; but even though true people, we say many things which we mean, but there is no depth of feeling, no potent emotion, no stirring of the heart's centre. Our Lord, when he said, "Ye shall be scattered; but after that I am risen, I will go before you into Galilee," spoke with a heavy heart, with many a melting sigh; and his whole soul went with the promise which closed the mournful scene. He has purchased what he promised, purchased it with his blood, and therefore he speaks most solemnly, and with his whole heart. There is no trifling on Christ's part with one to whom he makes a promise, and therefore he never forgets.

And, once more, *his honour is bound up with every promise.* If he had said that he would go to Galilee, and he had not gone, his disciples would have felt that he had made a mistake, or that he had failed. Brethren, if Christ's promise were to fail, what should we think of it? But he will never jeopardize his faithfulness and veracity.

> "As well might he his being quit,
> As break his promise or forget,"

Let the words of man be blown away like the chaff; but the words of Jesus must stand, for he will not tarnish his truth, which is one of the choicest of his crown-jewels.

I want you to turn over this thought in your quietude. Jesus remembers all that he has spoken; let not our hearts forget. Go to him with his covenant bonds and gracious promises: he will recognize his own signature. He will honour his own promises to the utmost, and none that trust in him shall complain of his having exaggerated.

I have done when I have said just this. I am very anxious that at this time we should come into real fellowship with Christ, at the table. Jesus, thou hast made us hunger after thee; wilt thou not feed us? Thou hast made us thirst after thee; wilt thou not supply that thirst? Do you think that our Beloved means to tantalize us? Our hunger is such that it would break through stone walls; shall we find his heart hard as a stone wall? No; he will clear the way, and we on our part will burst through all obstacles to come to him. "But," says one, "how can I come to him, poor, unknown, unworthy one that I am?" Such were the disciples at the lake. They were fishermen; and when he came to them, they had been toiling all night. Are you working for him? Then he will come to you. Expect him now. "Ah!" says one, "I have been working without success"—you are a poor minister whose congregation is falling off, whose church is not increased by conversions —you have toiled all the night, and taken nothing. Or you are a Sunday-school teacher, who cannot see her girls converted; or a brother who mourns that his boys are not coming to Christ. Well, I see who you are; you are just the sort of people that Jesus came to, for they had toiled all night in vain. Are you hungry? Jesus cries, "Children, have you any meat?" He comes to you and enquires about your hunger; while on the shore he has a fire of coals, and fish laid thereon, and bread. "Come and dine," says he. The table is spread. Come to himself! He is your food, your hope, your joy, your heaven. Come to him; give him no rest till he reveals himself to you, and you know of a surety that it is your Lord who embraces you. So may he do, to each of us just now, for his sweet love's sake! Amen.

12. The Evidence
of Our Lord's Wounds

"Then saith he to Thomas, Reach hither thy finger, and behold my hands; and reach hither thy hand, and thrust it into my side: and be not faithless, but believing."—John xx. 27.

AMONG us at this day we have many persons who are like Thomas—dubious, demanding signs and tokens, suspicious, and ofttimes sad. I am not sure that there is not a slight touch of Thomas in most of us. There are times and seasons when the strong man fails, and when the firm believer has to pause a while, and say, "Is it so?" It may be that our meditation upon the text before us may be of service to those who are touched with the malady which afflicted Thomas.

Notice, before we proceed to our subject in full, that *Thomas asked of our Lord what he ought not to have asked.* He wanted to put our risen Lord to tests which were scarcely reverent to his sacred person. Admire his Master's patience with him. He does not say, "If he does not choose to believe he may continue to suffer for his unbelief." But no; he fixes his eye upon the doubter, and addresses himself specially to him; yet not in words of reproach or anger. Jesus could bear with Thomas, though Thomas had been a long time with him, and had not known him. To put his finger into the print of the nails, and thrust his hand into his side, was much more than any disciple had a right to ask of his divine Master; and yet see the condescension of Jesus! Rather than Thomas should suffer from unbelief, Christ will let him take great liberties. Our Lord does not always act towards us according to his own dignity, but according to our necessity; and if we really are so weak that nothing will do but thrusting a hand into his side, he will let us do it. Nor do I wonder at this: if, for our sakes, he suffered a spear to be thrust there, he may well permit a hand to follow.

Observe that *Thomas was at once convinced.* He said: "My Lord, and my God." This shows our Master's wisdom, that he indulged him with such familiarity, because he knew that, though the demand was presumptuous, yet the act would work for his good. Our Lord sometimes wisely refuses—saying, "Touch me not; for I am not yet ascended"; but at other times, he wisely grants, because, though it be too much for us to ask, yet he thinks it wise to give.

The subject for our present meditation is just this: *the cure of doubts*. Thomas was permitted to put his finger into the print of the nails for the curing of his doubts. Perhaps you and I wish that we could do something like it. Oh, if our Lord Jesus would appear to me for once, and I might thrust my hand into his side; or, if I might for once see him, or speak with him, how confirmed should I be! No doubt that thought has arisen in the minds of many. We shall not have such proofs, my brethren, but we shall have something near akin to them, which will answer the same purpose.

I. The first head of my discourse shall be this: CRAVE NO SIGNS. If such signs be possible, crave them not. If there be dreams, visions, voices, ask not for them.

Crave not wonders, first, because *it is dishonouring to the sacred Word to ask for them.* You believe this Bible to be an inspired volume —the Book of God. The apostle Peter calls it "A more sure word of prophecy; whereunto ye do well that ye take heed." Are you not satisfied with that? When a person, in whose veracity you have the utmost confidence, bears testimony to this or that, if you straightway reply, "I would be glad of further evidence," you are slighting your friend, and casting unjust suspicion upon him. Will you cast suspicion upon the Holy Ghost, who, by this word, bears witness unto Christ? Oh, no! let us be content with his witness. Let us not wish to see, but remain satisfied to believe. If there be difficulties in believing, is it not natural there should be, when he that believes is finite, and the things to be believed are, in themselves, infinite? Let us accept the difficulties as being in themselves, in some measure, proofs of the correctness of our position, as inevitable attendants of heavenly mysteries, when they are looked at by such poor minds as ours. · Let us believe the Word, and crave no signs.

Crave no signs, because *it is unreasonable that we should desire more than we have already.* The testimony of the Lord Jesus Christ, contained in the Word, should alone suffice us. Beside that, we have the testimony of saints and martyrs, who have gone before us, dying triumphant in the faith. We have the testimony of many still among us, who tell us that these things are so. In part, we have the testimony of our own conscience, of our own conversion, of our own after-experience, and this is convincing testimony. Let us be satisfied with it. Thomas ought to have been content with the testimony of Mary Magdalene, and the other disciples, but he was not. We ought to trust our brethren's word. Let us not be unreasonable in craving after proofs when already proofs are afforded us without stint.

Crave no signs, because *it may be you will be presumptuous in so doing.* Who are you, to set God a sign? What is it he is to do before you will believe in him? Suppose he does not choose to do it, are you therefore arrogantly to say, "I refuse to believe unless the Lord will do my bidding"? Do you imagine that any angel would demean himself to pay attention to you, who set yourself up to make demands of the **Most High**? Assuredly not. It is presumption which dares to ask of God anything more than the testimony of himself which he chooses to grant us in his Word.

It is, moreover, damaging to ourselves to crave signs. Jesus says, "Blessed are they that have not seen, and yet have believed." Thomas had his sign, and he believed; and so far so good, but he missed a blessing peculiar to those who have not seen, and yet have believed. Do not, therefore, rob yourselves of the special favour which lights on those who, with no evidence but the witness of the Spirit of God, are prepared at once to believe in the Lord Jesus unto eternal life.

Again, crave no signs, for *this craving is highly perilous.* Translated according to many, and I think translated correctly, our Saviour said, "Reach hither thy finger, and put it into the print of the nails; and *become* not faithless, but believing," intending to indicate that Thomas, by degrees, would become faithless. His faith had grown to be so little that, if he continued insisting upon this and that, as a sign or evidence, that faith of his would get down to the very lowest; yea, he would have no faith left. "Become not faithless, but believing." Dear friends, if you began to seek signs, and if you were to see them, do you know what would happen? Why, you would want more; and when you had these, you would demand still more. Those who live by their feelings judge of the truth of God by their own condition. When they have happy feelings, then they believe; but if their spirits sink, if the weather happens to be a little damp, or if their constitution happens to be a little disordered, down go their spirits, and, straightway, down goes their faith. He that lives by a faith which does not rest on feeling, but is built upon the Word of the Lord, will remain fixed and steadfast as the mount of God; but he that craves for this thing and that thing, as a token for good at the hand of the Lord, stands in danger of perishing from want of faith. He shall not perish, if he has even a grain of living faith, for God will deliver him from the temptation; but the temptation is a very trying one to faith.

Crave, therefore, no sign. If you read a story of a person who saw a vision, or if you hear another declare that a voice spake to him—believe those things, or not, as you like; but do not desire them for yourself. These wonders may, or may not, be freaks of the imagination: I will not judge; but we must not rely upon them, for we are not to walk by sight, but by faith. Rely not upon anything that can be seen of the eyes, or heard of the ears; but simply trust him whom we know to be the Christ of God, the Rock of our salvation.

II. Secondly, when you want comfort, crave no sign, but TURN TO THE WOUNDS OF YOUR LORD. You see what Thomas did. He wanted faith, and he looked for it to Jesus wounded. He says nothing about Christ's head crowned with glory. He does not say that he must see him "girt about the paps with a golden girdle." Thomas, even in his unbelief, is wise; he turns to his Lord's wounds for comfort. Whenever your unbelief prevails, follow in this respect the conduct of Thomas, and turn your eyes straightway to the wounds of Jesus. These are the founts of never-failing consolation, from which, if a man doth once drink, he shall forget his misery, and remember his sorrow no more. Turn to the Lord's wounds; and if you do, what will you see?

First, you will see *the tokens of your Master's love.* O Lord Jesus,
what are these wounds in thy side, and in thy hands? He answers,
"These I endured when suffering for thee. How can I forget thee?
I have graven thee upon the palms of my hands. How can I ever fail
to remember thee? On my very heart the spear has written thy name."
Look at Jesus, dead, buried, risen, and then say, "He loved me, and
gave himself for me"! There is no restorative for a sinking faith like
a sight of the wounded Saviour. Look, soul, and live by the proofs
of his death! Come and put thy finger, by faith, into the print of
the nails, and these wounds shall heal thee of unbelief. The wounds
of our Lord are the tokens of his love.

They are, again, *the seals of his death,* especially that wound in his
side. He must have died; for "one of the soldiers, with a spear,
pierced his side, and forthwith came there out blood and water. And
he that saw it bare witness." The Son of God did assuredly die.
God, who made the heavens and the earth, took to himself our
nature, and in one wondrous person he was both God and man; and
lo! this wondrous Son of God bore sufferings unutterable, and consummated all by his death. This is our comfort, for if he died in our
stead, then we shall not die for our sins; our transgression is put
away, and our iniquity is pardoned. If the sacrifice had never been
slain, we might despair; but since the spear-wound proves that the
great Sacrifice really died, despair is slain, hope revives, and confidence rejoices.

The wounds of Jesus, next, are *the marks of identity.* By these we
identify his blessed person after his resurrection. The very Christ
that died has risen again. There is no illusion: there could be no
mistake. It is not somebody else foisted upon us in his place; but
Jesus who died has left the dead, for there are the marks of the
crucifixion in his hands and in his feet, and there is the spear-thrust
still. It is Jesus: this same Jesus. This is a matter of great comfort
to a Christian—this indisputably proven doctrine of the resurrection
of our Lord. It is the keystone of the gospel arch. Take that away,
or doubt it, and there remains nothing to console you. But because
Jesus died and in the selfsame person rose again, and ever lives,
therefore does our heart sweetly rest, believing that "them also which
sleep in Jesus will God bring with him"; and also that the whole of
the work of Jesus is true, is completed, and is accepted of God.

Again, those wounds, those scars of our Lord, were *the memorials of
his love to his people.* They set forth his love so that his chosen can
see the tokens; but they are also memorials to himself. He conde-
scendingly bears these as his reminders. In heaven, at this moment,
upon the person of our blessed Lord, there are the scars of his
crucifixion. Centuries have gone by, and yet he looks like a Lamb
that has been slain. Our first glance will assure us that this is he of
whom they said, "Crucify him; crucify him." Steadily look with the
eyes of your faith into the glory, and see your Master's wounds, and
say within yourself, "He has compassion upon us still: he bears the
marks of his passion." Look up, poor sufferer! Jesus knows what
physical pain means. Look up, poor depressed one! he knows what a
broken heart means. Canst thou not perceive this? Those prints upon

his hands, these sacred stigmata, declare that he has not forgotten what he underwent for us, but still has a fellow-feeling for us.

Once again, these wounds may comfort us because in heaven they are, before God and the holy angels, *the perpetual ensigns of his finished work*. That passion of his can never be repeated, and never needs to be: "After he had offered one sacrifice for sins for ever, he sat down on the right hand of God." But the memorials are always being presented before the infinite mind of God. Those memorials are, in part, the wounds in our Lord's blessed person. Glorified spirits can never cease to sing, "Worthy is the Lamb that was slain"; for every time they gaze upon him they perceive his scars. How resplendent shine the nail-prints! No jewels that ever gemmed a king can look one-half so lustrous as these. Though he be God over all blessed for ever, yet to us, at least, his brightest splendour comes from his death.

My hearer, whensoever thy soul is clouded, turn thou to these wounds which shine like a constellation of five bright stars. Look not to thine own wounds, nor to thine own pains, or sins, or prayers, or tears, but remember that "with his stripes we are healed." Gaze, then; intently gaze, upon thy Redeemer's wounds if thou wouldest find comfort.

III. This brings me to my third point, whenever faith is staggered at all, SEEK SUCH HELPS FOR YOUR FAITH AS YOU MAY. Though we cannot literally put our finger into the print of the nails, and may not wish to do so, yet let us use such modes of recognition as we do possess. Let us put these to their utmost use; and we shall no longer desire to put our hand into the Saviour's side. We shall be perfectly satisfied without that. Ye that are troubled with doubts and fears, I give you these recommendations.

First, if you would have your faith made vivid and strong, *study much the story of your Saviour's death*. Read it: read it: read it: read it. "*Tolle: lege*," said the voice to Augustine, "Take it: read it." So say I. Take the four evangelists; take the fifty-third chapter of Isaiah; take the twenty-second psalm; take all other parts of Scripture that relate to our suffering Substitute, and read them by day and by night, till you familiarize yourself with the whole story of his griefs and sin-bearing. Keep your mind intently fixed upon it; not sometimes, but continually. *Crux lux:* the cross is light. Thou shalt see it by its own light. The study of the narrative, if thou pray the Holy Ghost to enlighten thee, will beget faith in thee; and thou wilt, by its means, be very greatly helped, till, at last, thou wilt say, "I cannot doubt. The truth of the atonement is impressed upon my memory, my heart, my understanding. The record has convinced me."

Next, if this suffice not, *frequently contemplate the sufferings of Jesus*. I mean by that, when you have read the story, sit down, and try and picture it. Let your mind conceive it as passing before you. Put yourself into the position of the apostles who saw him die. No employment will so greatly strengthen faith, and certainly none will be more enjoyable!

> " Sweet the moments, rich in blessing,
> Which before the cross I spend,
> Life and health and peace possessing
> From the sinner's dying Friend."

An hour would be grandly spent if occupied in turning over each little detail, item, and incident in the marvellous death by which you are redeemed from death and hell. You will be surprised to find how this familiarizing of yourself with it, by the help of the Holy Spirit, will make it as vivid to you as if you saw it; and it will have a better effect upon your mind than the sight of it would have done; for probably the actual sight would have passed away from your mind, and have been forgotten, while the contemplation of the sorrowful scene will sink deep into your soul, and leave eternal lines! You will do well, first, to read and know the narrative, and then to contemplate it carefully and earnestly—I mean, not to think of it for a minute or two at chance times, but to take an hour or two that you can specially set apart on purpose to consider the story of your Saviour's death. I am persuaded, if you do this, it will be more helpful to you than putting his finger into the print of the nails was to Thomas.

What next? Why, dear friends, the Lord has a way of *giving his people wonderful realizations*. I hope I shall not say anything incorrect when I remark that there are times with us when the Lord is present with us, and we are strongly impressed with that fact, and therefore we act under a sense of that presence as if the divine glory were actually visible. Do you know what it is to write a letter to a friend feeling as if the Lord Jesus were looking over your shoulder? I know what it is at times to stand here and preach, and feel my Lord so near me that if I had literally seen him it would not have surprised me. Have you never, in the watches of the night, lain quiet when there was no sound but the ticking of the watch, and thought of your Lord till, though you knew there was no form before you, you were just as certain that he was there as if you could see his sorrowful countenance? In quiet places all alone—you scarcely like to tell the story—in the lone wood, and in the upper chamber—you have said, " If he spake I should not be more certain of his presence ; and if he smiled upon me I should not be surer of his love." These realizations have sometimes been so joyfully overwhelming that for years you have been lifted by them beyond all power of doubt. These holy summer days banish the frosts of the soul. Whenever a doubt is suggested to me about the existence of my Lord and Master, I feel that I can laugh the tempter to scorn, for I have seen him, and spoken with him. Not with these eyes, but with the eyes of my inner life, I have beheld my Lord, and communed with him. Wonder not that I am not among the crew of the black, piratical ship of " Modern Thought."

Nor is it merely in seasons of enjoyment that we get these helps, but in times of *deep distress*. Prostrate with pain, unable to enjoy any comfort, unable even to sleep, I have seen the soul of the believer as happy as if all sounds were marriage peals. Some of us know what it is to be right gleesome, glad, and joyous in hours of fierce trial, because Christ has been so near. In times of losses and bereavements, when the sorrow stung you to the quick, and you thought, before it came, that you never could bear it, yet have you been so sustained by a sight of the sacred head once wounded, and by fellowship with him in his sufferings, that you have said, " What are my griefs compared with.

his?" You have forgotten your sorrows and sung for joy of heart, as those that make merry. If you have been helped in this way, it will have all the effect upon you that ever could have come of putting your finger into the print of the nails. If, perchance, you have been given up to die, and have, mentally, gone through the whole process of dying, expecting soon to stand before the bar of God, and have been happy, and even exultant, then you could not doubt the reality of a religion that bore you up above the surging billows. Now that you are again restored to life for a little longer time, the recollection of your buoyant spirits, in what you thought to be your dying hours, will answer all the purpose to you, I think, of putting your finger into the nail-prints.

Sometimes the strengthening influence may be afforded under the stress of *temptation*. If ever, young man, you have had a strong temptation hurling itself against you, and your feet have almost gone —ay, let me not say "young man"; but if ever a man or a woman of any age has had to cry out, "God, help me: how shall I escape out of this?" and you have turned your eyes and seen your Lord and beheld his wounds; and if you have felt at that moment that the temptation had lost all power, you have had a seal from the Lord, and your faith has been confirmed. If at the sight of your Lord you have exclaimed, in presence of the temptation, "How can I do this great wickedness, and sin against God?" after that, you have had the best proof of your Redeemer's power to save. What better or more practical proof could you desire?

In these times, when the foundations of our faith are constantly being undermined, one is sometimes driven to say to himself, "Suppose it is not true." As I stood, the other night, beneath the sky, and watched the stars, I felt my heart going up to the great Maker with all the love that I was capable of. I said to myself, "What made me love God as I know I do? What made me feel an anxiety to be like him in purity? Whatever made me long to obey my God cannot be a lie." I know that it was the love of Jesus for me that changed my heart, and made me, though once careless and indifferent to him, now to pant with strong desires to honour him. What has done this? Not a lie, surely. A truth, then, has done it. I know it by its fruits. If this Bible were to turn out untrue, and if I died and went before my Maker, could I not say to him, "I believed great things of thee, great God; if it be not so, yet did I honour thee by the faith I had concerning thy wondrous goodness, and thy power to forgive"? and I would cast myself upon his mercy without fear. But we do not entertain such doubts; for those dear wounds continually prove the truth of the gospel, and the truth of our salvation by it. Incarnate Deity is a thought that was never invented by poet's mind, nor reasoned out by philosopher's skill. Incarnate Deity, the notion of the God that lived, and bled, and died in human form, instead of guilty man, it is itself its own best witness. The wounds are the infallible witness of the gospel of Christ.

Have you not felt those wounds very powerful to you in the form of *assistance in times of duty?* You said, "I cannot do it, it is too hard for me." You looked to Jesus wounded, and you could do anything. A sight of the bleeding Christ has often filled us with enthusiasm, and so with power : it has rendered us mighty with the omnipotence of God. Look at the church of Christ in all ages. Kings and princes did not know what to do with her. They vowed that they would destroy her. Their persecuting edicts went forth, and they put to death thousands upon thousands of the followers of Christ. But what happened? The death of Jesus made men willing to die for him. No pain, no torture, could keep back the believing host. They loved Jesus so that though their leaders fell by bloody deaths, another rank came on, and yet another, and another, till despots saw that neither dungeon, nor rack, nor fire could stop the march of the army of Christ. It is so now. Christ's wounds pour life into the church by transfusion : the life-blood of the church of God is from Jesus' wounds. Let us know its power and feel it working within us to will and to do of his good pleasure.

And as for those who do not trust him, what shall I say? The Lord help you to do so at once ; for as long as you do not trust him, you are under an awful curse, for it is written, "If any man love not the Lord Jesus, let him be Anathema Maranatha "—cursed at the coming of the Lord. May it not be so with you! Amen.

13. Mourning at the Sight of the Crucified

"And all the people that came together to that sight, beholding the things which were done, smote their breasts, and returned."—Luke xxiii. 48.

MANY in that crowd came together to behold the crucifixion of Jesus, in a condition of the most furious malice. They had hounded the Saviour as dogs pursue a stag, and at last, all mad with rage, they hemmed him in for death. Others, willing enough to spend an idle hour, and to gaze upon a sensational spectacle, swelled the mob until a vast assembly congregated around the little hill upon which the three crosses were raised. There unanimously, whether of malice or of wantonness, they all joined in mockery of the victim who hung upon the centre cross. Some thrust out the tongue, some wagged their heads, others scoffed and jeered, some taunted him in words, and others in signs, but all alike exulted over the defenceless man who was given as a prey to their teeth. Earth never beheld a scene in which so much unrestrained derision and expressive contempt were poured upon one man so unanimously and for so long a time. It must have been hideous to the last degree to have seen so many grinning faces and mocking eyes, and to have heard so many cruel words and scornful shouts. The spectacle was too detestable to be long endured of heaven. Suddenly the sun, shocked at the scene, veiled his face, and for three long hours the ribald crew sat shivering in midday midnight. Meanwhile the earth trembled beneath their feet, the rocks were rent, and the temple, in superstitious defence of whose perpetuity they had committed the murder of the just, had its holy veil rent as though by strong invisible hands. The news of this, and the feeling of horror produced by the darkness, and the earth-tremor, caused a revulsion of feelings; there were no more gibes and jests, no more thrustings out of the tongue and cruel mockeries, but they went their way solitary and alone to their homes, or in little silent groups, while each man after the manner of Orientals when struck with sudden awe, smote upon his breast. Far different was the procession to the gates of Jerusalem from that march of madness which had come out therefrom. Observe the power which God hath over human minds! See how he can tame the wildest, and make the most malicious and proud to cower down at his feet when he doth but manifest himself in the wonders of nature! How much more cowed and terrified will they be when he makes bare his arm and comes forth in the judgments of his wrath to deal with them according to their deserts!

This sudden and memorable change in so vast a multitude is the apt representative of two other remarkable mental changes. How like it is to the gracious transformation which a sight of the cross has often worked most blessedly in the hearts of men! Many have come under the sound of the gospel resolved to scoff, but they have returned to pray. The idlest and even the basest motives have brought men under the preaching, but when Jesus has been lifted up, they have been savingly drawn to him, and as a consequence have smitten upon their breasts in repentance, and gone their way to serve the Saviour whom they once blasphemed. Oh, the power, the melting, conquering, transforming power of that dear cross of Christ! My brethren, we have but to abide by the preaching of it, we have but constantly to tell abroad the matchless story, and we may expect to see the most remarkable spiritual results. We need despair of no man now that Jesus has died for sinners. With such a hammer as the doctrine of the cross, the most flinty heart will be broken; and with such a fire as the sweet love of Christ, the most mighty iceberg will be melted. We need never despair for the heathenish or superstitious races of men; if we can but find occasion to bring the doctrine of Christ crucified into contact with their natures, it will yet change them, and Christ will be their king.

A second and most awful change is also foretold by the incident in our text, namely, the effect which a sight of Christ enthroned will have upon the proud and obstinate, who in this life rebelled against him. Here they fearlessly jested concerning him, and insultingly demanded, "Who is the Lord, that we should obey him?" Here they boldly united in a conspiracy to break his bands asunder, and cast his cords from them, but when they wake up at the blast of the trump, and see the great white throne, which, like a mirror, shall reflect their conduct upon them, what a change will be in their minds! Where now your quibs and your jests, where now your malicious speeches and your persecuting words? What! Is there not one among you who can play the man, and insult the Man of Nazareth to his face? No, not one! Like cowardly dogs, they slink away! The infidel's bragging tongue is silent! The proud spirit of the atheist is broken; his blusterings and his carpings are hushed for ever! With shrieks of dismay, and clamorous cries of terror, they entreat the hills to cover them, and the mountains to conceal them from the face of that very Man whose cross was once the subject of their scorn. O take heed, ye sinners, take heed, I pray you, and be ye changed this day by grace, lest ye be changed by-and-by by terror, for the heart which will not be bent by the love of Christ, shall be broken by the terror of his name. If Jesus upon the cross do not save you, Christ on the throne shall damn you. If Christ dying be not your life, Christ living shall be your death. If Christ on earth be not your heaven, Christ coming from heaven shall be your hell. O may God's grace work a blessed turning of grace in each of us, that we may not be turned into hell in the dread day of reckoning.

We shall now draw nearer to the text, and in the first place, *analyse the general mourning around the cross;* secondly, we shall, if God shall help us, *endeavour to join in the sorrowful chorus;* and then, ere we conclude, we shall *remind you that at the foot of the cross our sorrow must be mingled with joy.*

1. First, then, let us ANALYSE THE GENERAL MOURNING which this text describes.

" All the people that came together to that sight, beholding the things which were done, smote their breasts, and returned." They all smote their breasts, but not all from the same cause. They were all afraid, not all from the same reason. The outward manifestations were alike in the whole mass, but the grades of difference in feeling were as many as the minds in which they ruled. There were many, no doubt, who were merely moved with a transient emotion. They had seen the death agonies of a remarkable man, and the attendant wonders had persuaded them that he was something more than an ordinary being, and therefore, they were afraid. With a kind of indefinite fear, grounded upon no very intelligent reasoning, they were alarmed, because God was angry, and had closed the eye of day upon them, and made the rocks to rend ; and, burdened with this indistinct fear, they went their way trembling and humbled to their several homes; but peradventure, ere the next morning light had dawned, they had forgotten it all, and the next day found them greedy for another bloody spectacle, and ready to nail another Christ to the cross, if there had been such another to be found in the land. Their beating of the breast was not a breaking of the heart. It was an April shower, a dewdrop of the morning, a hoar-frost that dissolved when the sun had risen. Like a shadow the emotion crossed their minds, and like a shadow it left no trace behind. How often in the preaching of the cross has this been the only result in tens of thousands ! In this house, where so many souls have been converted, many more have shed tears which have been wiped away, and the reason of their tears has been forgotten. A handkerchief has dried up their emotions. Alas ! alas ! alas ! that while it may be difficult to move men with the story of the cross to weeping, it is even more difficult to make those emotions permanent. "I have seen something wonderful, this morning," said one who had listened to a faithful and earnest preacher, "I have seen a whole congregation in tears." "Alas !" said the preacher, "there is something more wonderful still, for the most of them will go their way to forget that they ever shed a tear." Ah, my hearers, shall it be always so—always so ? Then, O ye impenitent, there shall come to your eyes a tear which shall drip for ever, a scalding drop which no mercy shall ever wipe away ; a thirst that shall never be abated; a worm that shall never die, and a fire that never shall be quenched. By the love you bear your souls, I pray you escape from the wrath to come !

Others amongst that great crowd exhibited emotion based upon more thoughtful reflection. They saw that they had shared in the murder of an innocent person. "Alas!" said they, " we see through it all now.

That man was no offender. In all that we have ever heard or seen of him, he did good, and only good: he always healed the sick, fed the hungry, and raised the dead. There is not a word of all his teaching that is really contrary to the law of God. He was a pure and holy man. We have all been duped. Those priests have egged us on to put to death one whom it were a thousand mercies if we could restore to life again at once. Our race has killed its benefactor." "Yes," saith one, "I thrust out my tongue, I found it almost impossible to restrain myself, when everybody else was laughing and mocking at his tortures; but I am afraid I have mocked at the innocent, and I tremble lest the darkness which God has sent was his reprobation of my wickedness in oppressing the innocent." Such feelings would abide, but I can suppose that they might not bring men to sincere repentance; for while they might feel sorry that they had oppressed the innocent, yet, perceiving nothing more in Jesus than mere mal-treated virtue and suffering manhood, the natural emotion might soon pass away, and the moral and spiritual result be of no great value. How frequently have we seen in our hearers that same description of emotion! They have regretted that Christ should be put to death, they have felt like that old king of France, who said, "I wish I had been there with ten thousand of my soldiers, I would have cut their throats sooner than they should have touched him;" but those very feelings have been evidence that they did not feel their share in the guilt as they ought to have done, and that to them the cross of Jesus was no more a saving spectacle than the death of a common martyr. Dear hearers, beware of making the cross to be a common-place thing with you. Look beyond the sufferings of the innocent manhood of Jesus, and see upon the tree the atoning sacrifice of Christ, or else you look to the cross in vain.

No doubt there were a few in the crowd who smote upon their breasts because they felt, "We have put to death a prophet of God. As of old our nation slew Isaiah, and put to death others of the Master's ser-vants, so to-day they have nailed to the cross one of the last of the prophets, and his blood will be upon us and upon our children." Peradventure some of them said, "This man claimed to be Messiah, and the miracles which attended his death prove that he was so. His life betokens it and his death declares it. What will become of our nation if we have slain the Prince of Peace! How will God visit us if we have put his prophet to death!" Such mourning was in advance of other forms; it showed a deeper thought and a clearer knowledge, and it may have been an admirable preparation for the after hearing of the gospel; but it would not of itself suffice as evidence of grace. I shall be glad if my hearers in this house to-day are persuaded by the character of Christ that he must have been a prophet sent of God, and that he was the Messiah promised of old; and I shall be gratified if they, therefore, lament the shameful cruelties which he received from our apostate race. Such emotions of compunction and pity are most commendable, and under God's blessing they may prove to be the fur-rows of your heart in which the gospel may take root. He who thus was cruelly put to death was God over all blessed for ever, the world's Redeemer, and the Saviour of such as put their trust in him. May you accept him to-day as your deliverer, and so be saved; for if not, the most virtuous regrets concerning his death, however much they may indicate your enlightenment, will not manifest your true conversion.

In the motley company who all went home smiting on their breasts, let us hope that there were some who said, " Certainly this was the Son of God," and mourned to think he should have suffered for their transgressions, and been put to grief for their iniquities. Those who came to that point were saved.   Blessed were the eyes that looked upon the slaughtered Lamb in such a way as that, and happy were the hearts that there and then were broken because he was bruised and put to grief for their sakes.   Beloved, aspire to this.   May God's grace bring you to see in Jesus Christ no other than God made flesh, hanging upon the tree in agony, to die, the just for the unjust, that we may be saved.   O come and repose your trust in him, and then smite upon your breasts at the thought that such a victim should have been necessary for your redemption; then may you cease to smite your breasts, and begin to clap your hands for very joy; for they who thus bewail a Saviour may rejoice in him, for he is theirs and they are his.

II. We shall now ask you TO JOIN IN THE LAMENTATION, each man according to his sincerity of heart, beholding the cross, and smiting upon his breast.

We will by faith put ourselves at the foot of the little knoll of Calvary: there we see in the centre, between two thieves, the Son of God made flesh, nailed by his hands and feet, and dying in an anguish which words cannot portray.   Look ye well, I pray you; look steadfastly and devoutly, gazing through your tears.   'Tis he who was worshipped of angels, who is now dying for the sons of men; sit down and watch the death of death's destroyer.   I shall ask you first to smite your breasts, as you remember that *you see in him your own sins*. How great he is!   That thorn-crowned head was once crowned with all the royalties of heaven and earth.   He who dies there is no common man.   King of kings and Lord of lords is he who hangs on yonder cross.   Then see the greatness of your sins, which required so vast a sacrifice.   They must be infinite sins to require an infinite person to lay down his life in order to their removal.   Thou canst never compass or comprehend the greatness of thy Lord in his essential character and dignity, neither shalt thou ever be able to understand the blackness and heinousness of the sin which demanded his life as an atonement. Brother, smite thy breast, and say, "God be merciful to me, the greatest of sinners, for I am such."   Look well into the face of Jesus, and see how vile they have made him !   They have stained those cheeks with spittle, they have lashed those shoulders with a felon's scourge; they have put him to the death which was only awarded to the meanest Roman slave; they have hung him up between heaven and earth, as though he were fit for neither; they have stripped him naked and left him not a rag to cover him!   See here then, O believer, the shame of thy sins.   What a shameful thing thy sin must have been; what a disgraceful and abominable thing, if Christ must be made such a shame for thee!   O be ashamed of thyself, to think thy Lord should thus be scorned and made nothing of for thee !   See how they aggravate his sorrows !   It was not enough to crucify him, they must insult him; nor that enough, they must mock his prayers and turn his dying cries into themes for jest, while they offer him vinegar to drink. See, beloved, how aggravated were your sins and mine! Come, my brother, let us both smite upon our breasts and say, "Oh, how our sins have piled up their guiltiness! It was not merely that we broke the law, but we sinned against light and knowledge; against rebukes and warnings. As his griefs are aggravated, even so are our sins!" Look still into his dear face, and see the lines of anguish which indicate the deeper inward sorrow which far transcends mere bodily pain and smart. God, his Father, has forsaken him. God has made him a curse for us. Then what must the curse of God have been against us? What must our sins have deserved? If when sin was only imputed to Christ, and laid upon him for awhile, his father turned his head away and made his Son cry out, "Lama Sabachthani!" Oh, what an accursed thing our sin must be, and what a curse would have come upon us; what thunderbolts, what coals of fire, what indignation, and wrath from the Most High must have been our portion had not Jesus interposed! If Jehovah did not spare his Son, how little would he have spared guilty, worthless men if he had dealt with us after our sins, and rewarded us according to our iniquities!

As we still sit down and look at Jesus, we remember that his death was voluntary—he need not have died unless he had so willed: here then is another striking feature of our sin, for our sin was voluntary too. We did not sin as of compulsion, but we deliberately chose the evil way. O sinner, let both of us sit down together, and tell the Lord that we have no justification, or extenuation, or excuse to offer, we have sinned wilfully against light and knowledge, against love and mercy. Let us smite upon our breasts, as we see Jesus willingly suffer, and confess that we have willingly offended against the just and righteous laws of a most good and gracious God. I could fain keep you looking into those five wounds, and studying that marred face, and counting every purple drop that flowed from hands and feet, and side, but time would fail us. Only that one wound—let it abide with you—smite your breast because you see in Christ your sin.

Looking again—changing, as it were, our stand-point, but still keeping our eye upon that same, dear crucified One, let us see there *the neglected and despised remedy for our sin.* If sin itself, in its first condition, as rebellion, bring no tears to our eyes, it certainly ought in *its* second manifestation, as ingratitude. The sin of rebellion is vile; but the sin of slighting the Saviour is viler still. He that hangs on the tree, in groans and griefs unutterable, is he whom some of you have never thought of, whom you do not love, to whom you never pray, in whom you place no confidence, and whom you never serve. I will not accuse you; I will ask those dear wounds to do it, sweetly and tenderly. I will rather accuse myself; for, alas! alas! there was a time when I heard of him as with a deaf ear; when I was told of him, and understood the love he bore to sinners, and yet my heart was like a stone within me, and would not be moved. I stopped my ear and would not be charmed, even with such a master-fascination as the disinterested love of Jesus. I think if I had been spared to live the life of an ungodly man, for thirty, forty, or fifty years, and had been converted at last, I should never have been able to blame myself sufficiently for rejecting Jesus during all those years. Why, even those of us who were converted in our youth, and almost in our childhood, cannot help blaming ourselves to think that so dear a friend, who had done so much for us, was so long slighted by us. Who could have done more for us than he, since he gave himself for our sins? Ah, how did we wrong him while we withheld our hearts from him! O ye sinners, how can ye keep the doors of your hearts shut against the Friend of Sinners? How can we close the door against him who cries, " My head is wet with dew, and my locks with the drops of the night: open to me, my beloved, open to me"? I am persuaded there are some here who are his elect: you were chosen by him from before the foundation of the world, and you shall be with him in heaven one day to sing his praises, and yet, at this moment, though you hear his name, you do not love him, and, though you are told of what he did, you do not trust him. What! shall that iron bar always fast close the gate of your heart? Shall that door still be always bolted? O Spirit of the living God, win an entrance for the blessed Christ this morning! If anything can do it, surely it must be a sight of the crucified Christ; that matchless spectacle shall make a heart of stone relent and melt, by Jesus' love subdued. O may the Holy Ghost work this gracious melting, and he shall have all the honour.

Still keeping you at the cross foot, dear friends, every believer here may well smite upon his breast this morning as he thinks of *who it was that smarted so upon the cross.* Who was it? It was he who loved us or ever the world was made. It was he who is this day the Bridegroom of our souls, our Best-beloved; he who has taken us into the banqueting house and waved his banner of love over us; he who has made us one with himself, and has vowed to present us to his Father without spot. It is he, our Husband, our Ishi, who has called us his Hephzibah because his soul delighteth in us. It is he who suffered thus for us. Suffering does not always excite the same degree of pity. You must know something of the individual before the innermost depths of the soul are stirred; and so it happens to us that the higher the character and the more able we are to appreciate it, the closer the relation and the more fondly we reciprocate the love, the more deeply does suffering strike the soul. You are coming to his table some of you to-day, and you will partake of bread: I pray you remember that it represents the quivering flesh that was filled with pain on Calvary. You will sip of that cup: then be sure to remember that it betokens to you the blood of one who loves you better than you could be loved by mother, or by husband, or by friend. O sit you down and smite your breasts that *he* should grieve; that heaven's Sun should be eclipsed; that heaven's Lily should be spotted with blood, and heaven's Rose should be whitened with a deadly pallor. Lament that perfection should be accused, innocence smitten, and love murdered; and that Christ, the happy and the holy, the ever blessed, who had been for ages the delight of angels, should now become the sorrowful, the acquaintance of grief, the bleeding and the dying. Smite upon your breasts, believers, and go your way!

Beloved in the Lord, if such grief as this should be kindled in you, it will be well to pursue the subject, and to reflect upon how unbelieving and how cruel we have been to Jesus since the day that we have known him. What, doth he bleed for me and have I doubted him? Is he the Son of God, and have I suspected his fidelity? Have I stood at the cross foot unmoved? Have I spoken of my dying Lord in a cold, indifferent spirit? Have I ever preached Christ crucified with a dry eye and a heart unmoved? Do I bow my knee in private prayer, and are my thoughts wandering when they ought to be bound hand and foot to his dear bleeding self? Am I accustomed to turn over the pages of the Evangelists which record my Master's wondrous sacrifice, and have I never stained those pages with my tears? Have I never paused spell-bound over the sacred sentence which recorded this miracle of miracles, this marvel of marvels? Oh, shame upon thee, hard heart! Well may I smite thee. May God smite thee with the hammer of his Spirit, and break thee to shivers. O thou stony heart, thou granite soul, thou flinty spirit, well may I strike the breast which harbours thee, to think that I should be so doltish in presence of love so amazing, so divine.

Brethren, you may smite upon your breasts as you look at the cross, and mourn that you should have done so little for your Lord. I think if anybody could have sketched my future life in the day of my conversion, and have said, "You will be dull and cold in spiritual things! and you will exhibit but little earnestness and little gratitude!" I should have said like Hazael, "Is thy servant a dog, that he should do this great thing?" I suppose I read your hearts when I say that the most of you are disappointed with your own conduct as compared with your too-flattering prophecies of yourselves! What! am I really pardoned? Am I in very deed washed in that warm stream which gushed from the riven side of Jesus, and yet am I not wholly consecrated to Christ? What! in my body do I bear the marks of the Lord Jesus, and can I live almost without a thought of him? Am I plucked like a brand from the burning, and have I small care to win others from the wrath to come? Has Jesus stooped to win me, and do I not labour to win others for him? Was he all in earnest about me, and am I only half in earnest about him? Dare I waste a minute, dare I trifle away an hour? Have I an evening to spend in vain gossip and idle frivolities? O my heart, well may I smite thee, that at the sight of the death of the dear Lover of my soul, I should not be fired by the highest zeal, and be impelled by the most ardent love to a perfect consecration of every power of my nature, every affection of my spirit, every faculty of my whole man? This mournful strain might be pursued to far greater lengths. We might follow up our confessions, still smiting, still accusing, still regretting, still bewailing. We might continue upon the bass notes evermore, and yet might we not express sufficient contrition for the shameful manner in which we have treated our blessed Friend.   We might say with one of our hymn writers—

> " Lord, let me weep for nought but sin,
>   And after none but thee ;
>   And then I would—O that I might—
>   A constant weeper be !"

One might desire to become a Niobe, and realise the desire of Jeremy, " O that my head were waters."   Even the holy extravagance of George Herbert does not surprise us, for we would even sing with him the song of GRIEF :—

> "Oh, who will give me tears?   Come, all ye springs,
>   Dwell in my head and eyes ; come, clouds and rain!
>   My grief hath need of all the wat'ry things
>   That nature hath produc'd.   Let ev'ry vein
>   Suck up a river to supply mine eyes,
>   My weary weeping eyes ; too dry for me,
>   Unless they get new conduits, new supplies,
>   To bear them out, and with my state agree.
>   What are two shallow fords, two little spouts
>   Of a less world?   The greater is but small.
>   A narrow cupboard for my griefs and doubts,
>   Which want provision in the midst of all.
>   Verses, ye are too fine a thing, too wise,
>   For my rough sorrows.   Cease! be dumb and mute;
>   Give up your feet and running to mine eyes,
>   And keep your measures for some lover's lute,
>   Whose grief allows him music and a rhyme ;
>   For mine excludes both measure, tune, and time.
>   —Alas, my God!"

III. Having, perhaps, said enough on this point—enough if God bless it, too much if without his blessing—let me invite you, in the third place, to remember that AT CALVARY, DOLOROUS NOTES ARE NOT THE ONLY SUITABLE MUSIC.

We admired our poet when, in the hymn which we have just sung, he appears to question with himself which would be the most fitting tune for Golgotha.

> " ' It is finished ;' shall we raise
>   Songs of sorrow or of praise ?
>   Mourn to see the Saviour die,
>   Or proclaim his victory ?
>
>   If of Calvary we tell,
>   How can songs of triumph swell ?
>   If of man redeemed from woe,
>   How shall notes of mourning flow ?"

He shows that since our sin pierced the side of Jesus, there is cause for unlimited lamentation, but since the blood which flowed from the wound has cleansed our sin, there is ground for unbounded

thanksgiving ; and, therefore, the poet, after having balanced the matter
in a few verses, concludes with—

> "'It is finished,' let us raise
> Songs of thankfulness and praise."

After all, you and I are not in the same condition as the multitude
who had surrounded Calvary; for at that time our Lord was still dead,
but now he is risen indeed. There were yet three days from that
Thursday evening (for there is much reason to believe that our Lord
was not crucified on Friday), in which Jesus must dwell in the
regions of the dead. Our Lord, therefore, so far as human eyes
could see him, was a proper object of pity and mourning, and not of
thanksgiving ; but now, beloved, he ever lives and gloriously reigns.
No charnel house confines that blessed body. He saw no corruption ;
for the moment when the third day dawned, he could no longer be held
with the bonds of death, but he manifested himself alive unto his disciples. He tarried in this world for forty days. Some of his time was
spent with those who knew him in the flesh ; perhaps a larger part of
it was passed with those saints who came out of their graves after his resurrection ; but certain it is that he is gone up, as the first-fruit from the
dead ; he is gone up to the right hand of God, even the Father. Do not
bewail those wounds, they are lustrous with supernal splendour. Do
not lament his death : he lives no more to die. Do not mourn that
shame and spitting :—

> " The head that once was crowned with thorns,
> Is crowned with glory now."

Look up and thank God that death hath no more dominion over him.
He ever liveth to make intercession for us, and he shall shortly come
with angelic bands surrounding him, to judge the quick and dead.
The argument for joy overshadows the reason for sorrow. Like as a
woman when the man-child is born remembereth no more her anguish,
for joy that a man is born into the world, so, in the thought of the
risen Saviour, who has taken possession of his crown, we will forget the
lamentation of the cross, and the sorrows of the broken heart of
Calvary.

Morever, hear ye the shrill voice of the high sounding cymbals, and
let your hearts rejoice within you, for in his death our Redeemer conquered all the hosts of hell. They came against him furiously, yea,
they came against him to eat up his flesh, but they stumbled and fell.
They compassed him about, yea, they compassed him about like bees ;
but in the name of the Lord did the Champion destroy them. Against
the whole multitude of sins, and all the battalions of the pit, the Saviour
stood, a solitary soldier fighting against innumerable bands, but he
has slain them all. " Bruised is the dragon's head." Jesus has led

captivity captive. He conquered when he fell; and let the notes of victory drown for ever the cries of sorrow.

Moreover, brethren, let it be remembered that men have been saved. Let there stream before your gladdened eyes this morning the innumerable company of the elect. Robed in white they come in long procession; they come from distant lands, from every clime; once scarlet with sin and black with iniquity, they are all white and pure, and without spot before the throne for ever; beyond temptation, beatified, and made like to Jesus. And how? It was all through Calvary. There was their sin put away; there was their everlasting righteousness brought in and consummated. Let the hosts that are before the throne, as they wave their palms, and touch their golden harps, excite you to a joy like their own, and let that celestial music hush the gentler voices which mournfully exclaim—

> " Alas! and did my Saviour bleed ?
> And did my Sovereign die ?
> Would he devote that sacred head
> For such a worm as I ? "

Nor is that all. You yourself are saved. O brother, this will always be one of your greatest joys. That others are converted through your instrumentality is occasion for much thanksgiving, but your Saviour's advice to you is, " Notwithstanding in this rejoice not, that the spirits are subject unto you; but rather rejoice, because your names are written in heaven." You, a spirit meet to be cast away, you whose portion must have been with devils—*you* are this day forgiven, adopted, saved, on the road to heaven. Oh! while you think that you are saved from hell, that you are lifted up to glory, you cannot but rejoice that your sin is put away from you through the death of Jesus Christ, your Lord.

Lastly, there is one thing for which we ought always to remember Christ's death with joy, and that is, that although the crucifixion of Jesus was intended to be a blow at the honour and glory of our God— though in the death of Christ the world did, so far as it was able, put God himself to death, and so earn for itself that hideous title, " a deicidal world," yet never did God have such honour and glory as he obtained through the sufferings of Jesus. Oh, they thought to scorn him, but they lifted his name on high! They thought that God was dishonoured when he was most glorified. The image of the Invisible, had they not marred it ? The express image of the Father's person, had they not defiled it ? Ah, so they said! But he that sitteth in the heavens may well laugh and have them in derision, for what did they? They did but break the alabaster box, and all the blessed drops of infinite mercy streamed forth to perfume all worlds. They did but rend the veil, and then the glory which had been hidden between the cherubim shone forth upon all lands. O nature, adoring God with thine ancient and priestly mountains, extolling him with thy trees, which clap their hands, and worshipping with thy seas, which in their fulness roar out Jehovah's praise; with all thy tempests and flames of fire, thy dragons and thy deeps, thy snow and thy hail, thou canst not glorify God as Jesus glorified him when he became obedient unto death. O heaven, with all thy jubilant angels, thine ever chanting cherubim and seraphim, thy thrice holy hymns, thy streets of gold and endless harmonies, thou canst not reveal the Deity as Jesus Christ revealed it on the cross. O hell, with all thine infinite horrors and flames unquenchable, and pains and griefs and shrieks of tortured ghosts, even thou canst not reveal the justice of God as Christ revealed it in his riven heart upon the bloody tree. O earth and heaven and hell! O time and eternity, things present and things to come, visible and invisible, ye are dim mirrors of the Godhead compared with the bleeding Lamb. O heart of God, I see thee nowhere as at Golgotha, where the Word incarnate reveals the justice and the love, the holiness and the tenderness of God in one blaze of glory. If any created mind would fain see the glory of God, he need not gaze upon the starry skies, nor soar into the heaven of heavens, he has but to bow at the cross foot and watch the crimson streams which gush from Immanuel's wounds. If you would behold the glory of God, you need not gaze between the gates of pearls, you have but to look beyond the gates of Jerusalem and see the Prince of Peace expire. If you would receive the noblest conception that ever filled the human mind of the lovingkindness and the greatness and the pity, and yet the justice and the severity and the wrath of God, you need not lift up your eyes, nor cast them down, nor look to paradise, nor gaze on Tophet, you have but to look into the heart of Christ all crushed and broken and bruised, and you have seen it all. Oh, the joy that springs from the fact that God has triumphed after all ! Death is not the victor ; evil is not master. There are not two rival kingdoms, one governed by the God of good, and the other by the God of evil; no, evil is bound, chained, and led captive ; its sinews are cut, its head is broken; its king is bound to the dread chariot of Jehovah-Jesus, and as the white horses of triumph drag the Conqueror up the everlasting hills in splendour of glory, the monsters of the pit cringe at his chariot wheels. Wherefore, beloved, we close this discourse with this sentence of humble yet joyful worship, "Glory be unto the Father, and to the Son, and to the Holy Ghost : as it was in the beginning is now and ever shall be, world without end. Amen.